Seekhna Band Toh Jeetna Band

Life lessons on growth, resilience, and leadership

Verses Kindler Publication

Verses Kindler Publication.

Website: www.verseskindlerpublication.com

Seekhna Band Toh Jeetna Band

By: Mr. Vivek Agrawal

ISBN: 978-93-49532-75-5

FICTION STORIES 1st Edition

Price: INR 499/$22

Disclaimer

Seekhna Band Toh Jeetna Band is written by Mr. Vivek Agrawal. The entirety of this published work comprises the original content of the author, who has undertaken diligent efforts in its editing. The characters depicted herein may be fictitious or inspired by real events; however, they are not intended to cause offense or represent any prejudice against any caste or system. Any similarity to the names of actual individuals, locations, or institutions is purely coincidental and serves the narrative. The author bears sole responsibility for the originality of this work; the publisher assumes no liability thereof.

Table of Contents

Preface 7

Foreword 15

About Me 19

Chapter 1: Early Childhood Served as a Foundation 23

Chapter 2: Schooling and Teenage 33

Chapter 3: Stepping into Engineering Without a Background in Computers 54

Chapter 4: Dealing with Cancellation of College Affiliation 75

Chapter 5: The MBA Shift & Recession-Era Struggles 86

Chapter 6: Rise in the Corporate World 105

Chapter 7: From Overwhelmed Manager to Strategic Leader: A Coaching Transformation Story 120

Chapter 8: Core Principles & Mindset 134

Chapter 9: Moments of Doubt vs. Moments of Triumph 159

Chapter 10: Advice for the Young Dreamers 170

Chapter 11: Looking Inward & Looking Ahead 186

Chapter 12: Introspective Prompts to Ignite Your Transformation 198

The Journey Never Ends: And The Learning Continues... 209

Preface

"Life is 10% what happens to us and 90% how we react to it."

– Charles R. Swindoll

Not all stories begin in glossy boardrooms or behind the gates of elite institutions. Some take root in small towns, in modest homes, where dreams are shaped by grit, not privilege. Mine is one such story.

Acknowledgements

This book is not just my story—it is the reflection of every person, moment, and force that has shaped me. It is built on the values I inherited, the people who stood by me, and the lessons I've gathered along the way. I offer this section as a humble note of gratitude.

To the Roots of My Values

I begin by expressing my deepest respect and gratitude to my grandfather, Late Shri Shiv Prakash Agrawal.

He was the moral compass of our family—the ceiling of our values. His quiet strength, deep wisdom, and unwavering integrity continue to echo in my thoughts and actions, even today. The foundation of who I am was laid by the life he lived, and I hope this book honors that legacy.

To My Parents – My First Teachers

To my parents, Shri Bishnu Kant Agrawal & Smt Indu Rani Agrawal, who brought me into this world and raised me with unwavering dedication and care.

They never let me stray from the path of righteousness. They taught me right from wrong, how to speak with respect, how to carry myself with humility, and how to stay grounded in values—

even in moments of chaos. Their presence has been my compass, gently but firmly guiding me through life.

To My Life Partner

To my wife, Ekta Agrawal, whose selfless love and unwavering belief in me has been the bedrock of my professional and personal life.

Her patience, strength, and support made it possible for me to pursue my ambitions. Behind every success I've had, she has stood quietly, making sacrifices most will never see, but which I will never forget.

To My Children – My Light

To my children, Aaradhya & Jaanvi who have been my motivation and my grounding force.

Their smiles have lifted me in my darkest hours. Their presence reminds me why I do what I do. They are my reason to stay humble, hopeful, and forward-looking.

To My Sister – My Lifelong Ally

To my sister, Sneha Saurabh, who, no matter how grown-up or accomplished, has always remained my little sister—caring, wise, and full of heart.

She's been the person I could lean on, open up to, and rely on for both perspective and warmth. Her quiet strength has lit the path ahead of me more times than I can count.

To the Teachers Who Shaped Me

To Miss Mrinalini, whose guidance in my early school years gave me a strong start.

To Ms. Thomas, who mentored me from Class 8 to Class 12 and played a major role in shaping my discipline and character.

To Kamal Nayan Sir, who was more than a teacher—he was a guide, a friend, a mentor at home. He taught me, studied with me, and helped me grow beyond academics.

To Mr. Tebriwal, who taught me resilience through his example and presence.

Each of them helped shape the mindset I carry even today.

To My Mentor During MBA – Prof. S. K. Gupta

To Prof. S. K. Gupta, my mentor during my MBA days, I owe a special debt of gratitude.

He was the one who stood the strongest for me when I faced some of the most difficult situations of my life. His unwavering faith, guidance, and quiet strength gave me the courage to hold on when everything else seemed uncertain.

He not only guided me academically but also shaped my moral compass. It was under his influence that I learned the true *art and value of honesty*—a virtue that became one of the strongest pillars of my life and continues to guide me every single day.

Had it not been for him, I would not be who I am today. His lessons live within me, and his impact will stay with me till my last breath.

To Friends, Colleagues, and Teams

To my college friends, office colleagues, and professional teams—thank you for the support, the camaraderie, and the environment that shaped my evolution.

To the friends who stood by me during highs and lows, who listened without judgment, who believed in me even when I doubted myself—thank you. You've been my anchor in the storm.

To My Professional Mentors and Team

To Mr. Dinesh Agarwal, my ex-boss and the CEO of IndiaMART—thank you for being my guardian at work.

You challenged me, pushed me into the most difficult problems, and showed me what leadership under pressure really means. Your belief in me became the foundation of my growth into a CIO.

To my team at IndiaMART, thank you for your commitment, your energy, and your willingness to dream big and do what it takes. You helped make impossible goals possible.

To all the colleagues and leaders who walked with me—thank you for the trust, the friction, the learning, and the shared wins.

To My Coach and Inner Guide

To Mr. Dhruv Prakash Agarwal, my coach and mentor during a significant chapter of my career—thank you for always holding the mirror to my strengths.

In moments of self-doubt, you reminded me of what I was capable of. Your presence gave me confidence and the energy to keep moving forward.

To My Coaching Tribe

To my coaching clients, thank you for trusting me with your journeys.

To the ICF community, thank you for giving me a platform to grow and for shaping my evolution as a coach and a human being. Coaching has not only made me better at helping others—it has helped me understand myself at a much deeper level.

To the Team Behind the Book

To my editor and publisher, thank you for helping me shape these scattered thoughts into a cohesive narrative.

Your guidance turned this dream into something real, and readable. You've helped make this book not just a personal milestone, but a meaningful offering.

To You, the Reader

To every reader who picked up this book—thank you.

Thank you for investing your time in my story. I hope you found a part of yourself in these pages, and I hope it leaves you with something you can carry forward in your own journey.

And Finally, To the One Above

Above all, I bow my head in gratitude to God, who has always shown me the way.

In moments of confusion, I found clarity. In moments of struggle, I found strength. Every detour led to a deeper destination, and every failure brought hidden blessings. His grace has been my silent partner, and for that, I remain forever grateful.

Foreword

When I began writing Seekhna Band Toh Jeetna Band, it was not with the intention of becoming an author. It was with the intention of pausing, looking back at my own journey, and acknowledging the people, lessons, and struggles that shaped who I am today.

From my early childhood in Begusarai, where discipline and values became my foundation, to the love and sacrifices of my parents, who taught me resilience and service before I even knew the words, my life has been guided by anchors I carry even today. My mother's influence on my mindset and my father's example of simplicity and kindness remain the compass I turn to in moments of doubt.

Along the way, mentors, teachers, colleagues, and later, my coaches, helped me see parts of myself I had overlooked. Their encouragement taught me that growth is rarely a straight line; it is a journey of stumbles, pauses, and breakthroughs.

This book is a tribute to all those voices, moments, and nudges that reminded me to keep learning. It is not just a collection of stories from my life; it is a reminder that when we stop learning, we stop living fully.

My hope is that as you turn these pages, you will find pieces of your own journey reflected here; and that you will give yourself permission to learn, unlearn, and relearn as often as life demands.

Because in the end, winning is not about trophies or titles; it is about the courage to keep growing.

This is my journey so far. And it is also an invitation for you to reflect on yours.

— Vivek Agrawal

Dedicated to my parents, mentors, and everyone who taught me the power of learning.

About Me

Hello! I'm Vivek Agrawal. I was born in Begusarai, Bihar, where power cuts were frequent, but ambition never flickered. I didn't inherit a blueprint for success. No mentors from Silicon Valley. No crash courses in leadership. What I had was curiosity, resilience, and a belief that learning never fails those who persist.

From that dusty town in Bihar, life took me on a journey I could have never scripted. I eventually rose to become the Chief Information Officer at IndiaMART, India's largest B2B marketplace, leading hundreds of professionals through digital transformation. Today, I'm a Certified Coach who creates a reflective space for individuals to think deeply, unlock their potential, and navigate through the very challenges I once learned to overcome.

This book isn't about podium speeches or boardroom buzzwords. It's about leadership that's lived, shaped in moments of doubt, refined in failures, and grounded in values. I've learned that real leadership has very little to do with control and everything to do with connection. It's about asking better questions, embracing uncertainty, and showing up with integrity even when things don't go your way.

At IndiaMART, I had the privilege of growing up in an environment where change wasn't feared; it was welcomed. I led digital initiatives, built high-performing teams, and worked shoulder-to-shoulder with the CEO and executive leadership to steady the ship during storms and scale it during surges. Through it all, one lesson stood tall: the culture you nurture determines the future you build.

Leadership, I've come to believe, is not a god-gifted skill. It's a discipline, rooted in service, elevated by empathy, and sustained by self-awareness.

And that's what led me to write this book.

Why I Wrote This Book

I believe the future will be shaped not just by technology or talent, but by leadership, the kind that begins within. This book was created out of real experiences and reflection, as a guide, a friend, and a map for any person who is beginning their journey into leadership.

Today, change is constant, competition is high, pressure to "succeed" is high, and with all of this, it is easy to feel overwhelmed and lost. Easy to doubt yourself. Easy to wonder if you're enough.

But here's what I've learned, leadership isn't a position you wait for. It's a mindset you choose.

This book is a must-read for:

- The students who are told to follow the crowd but feel the urge to carve their own path.
- The young professionals who are trying to find meaning in their careers and courage in their choices.

- The aspiring leaders who don't just want to make a living, they want to make a difference.

It is my way of reaching out and saying: You don't have to have it all figured out to lead. You just need the courage to begin.

The stories and lessons within these pages are not drawn from management books or fancy seminars. They're forged in real-world challenges, late-night decisions, team conflicts, failures that stung, and wins that came only after a struggle. Through it all, I discovered that leadership is not about control, but about clarity. Not about having all the answers, but about asking the right questions.

And those are the questions I hope this book will spark in you.

If you read with an open heart and a curious mind, this book will help you:

- Lead yourself before you lead others
- Build confidence where there is doubt
- Turn fear into fuel for action
- And navigate your journey with purpose and authenticity

Because the world doesn't just need more managers or experts.

It calls for leaders, bold, empathetic, and resilient. Leaders who fearlessly embrace growth, rise above setbacks, and stand strong after every fall.

And that leader is already within you. This book is just a mirror to help you see it more clearly.

If I could do it, you can too. So, let's awaken the leader in you.

- Vivek Agrawal

Leadership Coach | Ex-CIO, IndiaMART

Digital Transformation Advisor | Lifelong Learner

Chapter 1: Early Childhood Served as a Foundation

I was born in 1983 in Begusarai, a town lying close to Patna in Bihar. Technically, it is my birthplace, but the genesis of my narrative is more deep-seated, cutting across generations and geographies. Begusarai was the polestar of our family in the 1960s when my grandfather moved there from Baggar, a small town close to Jhunjhunu in Rajasthan. He was a Marwari by birth, rooted in tradition, hard work, and community. Like most Marwaris of his time, he looked for opportunities away from the desert terrain of Rajasthan, and Begusarai, with its growing industrial presence and proximity to trading routes, appeared to be a land of promise.

He established our first business there, an andi mill, a tiny unit for processing oil, which over the years grew to become an enterprise that exported goods to other regions of the country. Calcutta, as it was called at that time, was our key market. And of course, with business increasing, the family expanded. My father and mother finally settled in Calcutta during the early 1980s, when they felt that life presented improved opportunities and a firmer educational background for their children. I was just two years old when we migrated from Begusarai to the metropolis, but the town was perfectly fit in our memories, forever overshadowing us like a second home we never really abandoned.

We had a simple but spacious four-room apartment in Calcutta. Life there was routine, disciplined, and cordial. Though I was too young to hold onto vivid memories of those early years, some memories lingered, such as the yellow school buses I rode to school, the reassuring hands of my parents as they escorted me to the bus stop, or the steep stairway in my school building that my little legs wouldn't reach the top of. My mother still remembered that I would frequently not want to go up by myself, and the bus of school bus, whether a teacher or staff member, would have to carry me up, laughing at my refusal to go.

I attended a junior Hindi high school in Calcutta, whose ironic naming was that although it was called thus, it was actually one of the better-known schools in the district. My school days are few, but I have a distinct recollection of the cadence of our daily rhythm. We were an early-to-bed-and-early-to-rise household, perhaps one of the best things that my childhood ever taught me. We'd all be asleep by 8 or 8:30 at night and up by 4:30 or 5 in the morning. My body clock has served me this way ever since. Even now, I wake up at 3:30 or 4 a.m., a second-nature habit. Discipline was not taught to me in terms of orders; it was lived around me, quietly, regularly, and with love.

My mother was instrumental in moulding the student I turned out to be. During exams, she would sit with me at dawn, quietly assisting me to rework what I had learned the previous day. Her patience was limitless, her strength silent but powerful. I didn't realize it at the time, but now, in hindsight, I know that much of what I am today, my inner calm, my compassion, and even my capacity to cope with stress, was shaped by her firm hand. My father was the very definition of punctuality. If a meeting was scheduled for noon, he would make sure he not only made it on time but early, with some allowance for every eventuality, even if it meant showing up at 11:55 and waiting. Whether he had to travel three floors or had a longer journey, his timing was always precise. I understood that punctuality wasn't merely about showing up on time; it was about being reliable.

Even with this disciplined life, Calcutta never quite belonged to me. Our flat, comfortable as it was, remained sometimes a cage. I could not go downstairs alone. My excursions were always family-bound, ordered, and secure. I did not realize it at the time, but a hunger for liberty, for rough skies and sloppy afternoons, had been quietly growing within me.

It was in 1995 that this hunger found its homecoming.

My grandfather, who had remained behind in Begusarai all these years to manage the family business, had grown old and isolated. He wrote to my father, or maybe it was a call; the sequence of events is fuzzy, but his words were unmistakable: he needed us. And so, my parents made up their minds to return to Begusarai. I was in Class 6 at the time, having done my primary school in Calcutta.

That transformation, geographical, emotional, and cultural, meant a great deal. From the congestion and restrictiveness of Calcutta to the wider, earthier world of Begusarai, my existence changed course. I received admission to St. Paul's School, which was right in the vicinity of our house. I was now immersed in a slower-moving world, but one which provided room to discover, both in the physical environment around me and in my growing sense of self.

Between 1995 and 2002, I remained in Begusarai and pursued my education up to Class 12. Those seven years changed me in ways that I'm still unearthing. My schedule remained disciplined, early to sleep, early to wake up, but now it had a different zing. I wasn't restricted anymore. I could wander a bit, get some sun on my face in the mornings, and hear the sound of temple bells ringing in the distance, or even go to my grandfather's mill, which continued to run, albeit on a smaller scale. It was like entering into a heritage, a tale I had been born with but only now starting to grasp.

My relationship with my parents was as close as ever. If the quiet strength was my mother, the structured foundation was my father. There was just so much love in our home, and discipline as well, but never forced. It was packaged with love. We didn't just hear how to live; we watched it lived out daily. I marveled at my father's precision and my mother's wisdom. Her voice was never loud, but it hung around longer than most. She didn't lecture, but her choices, always considered, never on the spur of the moment, showed me what grace under pressure was.

Much of my childhood self was also formed because of my sister. Four years my junior, she was at once my responsibility and friend. We were close. I was watchful, perhaps overbearing as older brothers tend to be, but she never grumbled. We played, quarrelled, laughed, and stood up for one another. Even now, I believe that those early attachments of love and concern have enriched us emotionally as human beings.

Religion and tradition were an essential part of our home. We weren't merely culturally Marwari; we lived it out. Festivals were observed with rituals, not fanfare alone. My grandfather especially clung tenaciously to the customs and principles of our forefathers. Observing him perform his morning prayers, keep meticulous books of the family business, or even just talk in his gentle Marwari-accented Hindi made me feel like lineage, like I was a tiny piece of a very long chain. It wasn't something that weighed upon me; rather, it grounded me. It reminded me who I was, where I was from, and what values I passed on.

By the time 2002 rolled in, I had finished my Class 12, and it was time to relocate again, this time from Begusarai. That new chapter would transport me into the broader world, but the foundation had been set. Whether it was the small, cosy flat in Calcutta or the open spaciousness of life in Begusarai, my childhood had provided me with something priceless: a sense of discipline, love, and identity. I had been given the best of both worlds, the disciplined ambition of a city life and the grounded peace of a small town's existence.

In retrospect, I now understand that those early years were not merely about the places I stayed. They were about people, their choices, their sacrifices, and their unseen strings of love that established the structure for the person I would one day become.

Some values take root before you even realize they've become a part of you. For me, that began in Calcutta during the vibrant swirl of Durga Puja. The city would transform into a living celebration, every lane adorned with lights, every corner echoing with the sound of the dhols. Pandal-hopping with my sister and father remains one of my earliest, most vivid memories.

We would go from one mandap to another, marvelling at the goddess in all her grand manifestations. I remember standing quietly in front of the idol, joining my hands the way my father did. It was through him that I first learned about the nine forms of Durga, the Navadurga. Not from a textbook, but from his stories and the reverence in his voice. Those rituals weren't just about worship; they were early lessons in faith, discipline, and the quiet strength of tradition.

Even while we lived in Calcutta, we visited Begusarai once a year, usually during winter vacations. But summer was always reserved for Allahabad, my maternal grandparents' home. That one-month break was our joyful escape. My five maternal uncles, mamas, and their children would gather under one roof, creating a happy chaos only a large Indian family can offer. Those summer days were filled with laughter, games, mangoes, and mischief.

The house itself was special. A multi-floor bungalow with a sprawling temple on the ground floor. My Nana ji had a shop where he sold gold ornaments, was also the temple's caretaker. He would wake up every morning at 4 a.m., sweep the floors, light the lamps, and perform the aarti, all before heading off to work. And in those silent, sacred hours, I would be right beside him.

I was always an early riser, even then. So while the rest of the house slept, I would help Nana ji clean, arrange the flowers, and assist in the rituals. I didn't know it then, but those moments shaped a deep bond with discipline and devotion, two themes that would keep recurring throughout my life. It wasn't just about religion. It was about being present, being useful, and being connected.

I was often praised by my relatives for these small acts. It felt good, yes, but more than that, it gave me a sense of belonging and purpose. And when you're a child, being seen and appreciated for who you are is everything. That's when I began to understand: when you're sincere, the world notices, even if you don't speak much.

Because truth be told, I was always an introvert. Quiet, observant, never the loudest voice in the room. Even today, I consider myself one. I speak only when needed, and I prefer listening over talking. Not because I lack opinions, but because I've always believed that words should carry weight, not just volume.

This habit of speaking less, I think, grew naturally with me. My father, too, wasn't someone who indulged in unnecessary talk. And perhaps that quietness filtered down. But what I lacked in words, I made up for in consistency and presence. Whether it was in school, family rituals, or casual gatherings, I was always around, always attentive.

In 1995, we moved permanently to Begusarai. I had just completed Class 5. And while the shift was practical, my ageing grandfather needed us; it turned out to be deeply transformative for me.

Begusarai wasn't like Calcutta. It was open, sprawling, and rural in the best way. We lived on the outskirts, in a farmhouse-style bungalow surrounded by fields, trees, and silence. After the boxed-in feeling of our flat in Calcutta, this space felt like freedom.

My grandfather made sure I felt that, too. One of the first things he did was get me a bicycle. Not just any bicycle, but my first one. It became my ticket to joy. Since stepping out beyond the premises wasn't always safe, I'd ride endlessly inside our campus. Our bungalow was in one corner, and the factory's office was in another, so my route was set. I'd zoom from one end to the other, imagining adventures in between.

My mother would often recall how I used to say that Calcutta was like a jungle, always boxed in. But here, here I could feel the wind, touch the grass, see the stars. That freedom gave me room to think, to imagine, and to grow.

Behind our home was a garden, not just a decorative one with flowers, but a true *kitchen garden*. Vegetables, fruits, herbs, and most of what we ate came from our own backyard. I would often help in picking fresh greens, sometimes even getting scolded for plucking things before they were ripe. But those small chores taught me the value of self-sufficiency, of staying connected to the land and what it gave us.

There was no shortage of love in Begusarai. My grandfather, having insisted we return, was determined to make it worth our while. He encouraged me to explore, to enjoy, to learn. And I did. Within those boundaries, I was entirely free. I was never forced to be someone I wasn't. But there were two expectations: be disciplined and treat everyone with respect. That was non-negotiable. And those two simple instructions became the moral compass of my life.

When I joined St. Paul's School in Class 6, I began my academic chapter in Begusarai. I still remember Ms. Mrinalini, her gentle face, her kind but firm voice. She liked me. Most teachers did. I was never the loud kid, but I was present. Always sitting in the front row, always attentive. Chubby, shy, quiet, but helpful. I would carry books, help arrange the classroom, or clean the blackboard. These little things meant a lot back then. They still do.

Though I wasn't the class topper, I was always among the top few, floating somewhere between ranks one, two, or three. I liked studying. But more than that, I liked the structure. I liked knowing what was expected of me, and then doing it well. That feeling of being useful, dependable, anchored me.

In Class 8, something changed. Our class teacher was Ms. Sarama Jannet Thomas, a woman of great discipline. She was strict, yes, but also fair and encouraging. She didn't tolerate nonsense, and somehow, I found myself aligned with her values. In many ways, she reminded me of my father, firm, precise, and quietly compassionate. Under her watch, my own sense of order deepened.

Being in a Catholic school added another layer to this discipline. From morning prayers to perfectly aligned uniforms, from punctuality to politeness, everything was designed to build character. And for someone like me, who already valued structure, this became a natural extension of what I had been learning at home.

Looking back now, I can see it clearly: those years in Begusarai weren't just about academics or festivals. They were about becoming. About shaping the raw material of childhood into the early mould of the man I would later become.

The values I live by today, discipline, respect, quiet integrity, they didn't arrive one day. They were whispered into my life over time. Through early mornings with Nana ji, through temple rituals with my father, through classroom discipline with Ms. Sarama, through cycling across our factory compound, and through every unsaid word that still carried meaning.

In hindsight, it all seems so intentional. But in the moment, it was just life unfolding, gently, quietly, faithfully.

Chapter 2: Schooling and Teenage

Ms. Thomas was more than just a teacher to me; she was a role model. Whenever I needed help, guidance, or clarity, she was my go-to person in school. Her presence brought a certain reassurance. I knew if something troubled me, she'd listen and offer direction without judgment. That kind of trust doesn't come easily, but with her, it was natural.

The other figure I deeply admired in school was our principal, Mr. Abishai. We called him Abishai Sir; he had a head of white hair and a calm but powerful demeanor. He led the school with quiet strength. He was strict, yes, but also soft-spoken and kind. I didn't interact with him often, but he knew me. I knew him. And that mutual awareness created an unspoken bond of respect. He knew I was a quiet student, serious, disciplined, and helpful. And I knew he valued those traits.

My sister and I both studied at the same school. She had joined Class 2 when I came into Class 6. Over the years, as she grew up, she, too, came under the guidance of Ms. Thomas. Both of us were known for our discipline. We received awards for maintaining the best uniform, for being helpful, and for overall conduct. I still remember standing on stage receiving the award for the most disciplined student in Class 9 or 10. Those recognitions meant a lot at that age; they quietly shaped our confidence.

Ms. Thomas, being very particular about rules and behavior, was not liked by everyone. Her strictness clashed with many students, especially in a place like Bihar, where the local culture sometimes reflected casualness in language or behavior. She stood her ground. And because I shared her values, discipline, respect, and seriousness, she saw in me a reflection of her ideals. It's true, she favored me. And while that made some of my classmates jealous, I didn't feel bad about it. I believed then, and I believe now, that if you're on the right path and someone appreciates you for it, it's a blessing.

When I think back on my schooling years in Begusarai, there's one name that rises quietly but firmly above the noise of classrooms, corridors, school assemblies, and exam report cards: Mr. Kamal NayanNain, or as we fondly called him, Kamal Sir.

Our paths crossed in 1995, just as I had stepped into Class 6 and our family had moved to Begusarai. That was also the time we brought home our first computer. The excitement in the house was electric. A computer, in those days, was still a novelty. A piece of magic. And with that magic machine came the man who would become one of the most formative influences of my life.

Kamal Sir came to teach us computers, but very soon, he became far more than just a computer teacher. He became a steady presence, first in the background, and eventually in the foreground of my life. What started as weekly computer lessons slowly evolved into something much deeper: he began helping me with studies wherever I needed support. But even that doesn't quite capture what he became.

He was not a tutor, not in the traditional sense. He was a teacher, yes, but also a guide, a mentor, and at times, even a companion in play. We didn't just study together; we played cricket, had conversations, and shared a friendship that transcended the typical student-teacher relationship. For those six years, from Class 6 to Class 12, he was a part of my everyday rhythm.

His role in my academics was particularly significant until Class 10. And though his active involvement in my studies tapered off after that, the foundation he helped lay remained rock solid. He never taught to tick a syllabus box. His approach was organic, full of warmth and insight. He made learning feel effortless, even joyful. I often believe that the confidence I carried into Class 10 and 12 was built in those early evenings, sitting in our home in Begusarai, learning not just lessons from books, but also lessons of life from him.

The results spoke for themselves. I secured 81% in Class 10 and 88% in Class 12, scores that made many in Begusarai sit up and take notice. And in that small-town ecosystem, word spreads fast. Soon, Kamal Sir was known across Begusarai, not just as a teacher, but as "the tuition master who made Vivek." His reputation soared. But through it all, he remained the same, humble to the core, with a heart full of grace and a presence that never sought the limelight.

In hindsight, it's not just his academic inputs that made the difference. It was his *humility*, his *consistency*, and the quiet, dependable way in which he showed up for me, day after day, year after year. And those qualities have stayed with me. They've become my compass in how I try to show up for others now, as a father, a professional, and a lifelong learner.

What's even more beautiful is that our connection didn't end when I left Begusarai. Years later, when life had moved on and I had a family of my own, Kamal Sir moved to Delhi–Noida, close to where I live now. And in what feels like a full-circle moment, he now teaches my own children, my 8-year-old daughter and 13-year-old son.

There's something deeply emotional about that. The same man who once guided me through the tricky terrains of school life is now holding the hands of my children, teaching them not just how to learn, but how to enjoy the process. It's rare to see someone's influence travel across generations like this.

To describe him in words feels limiting. But if I had to try, I'd say this: he is humility personified. A quiet light. A gentle force. Someone who never needed to speak too loudly to make an impact. And someone whose presence in my life continues to be a gift I treasure.

When I shared the earlier chapters, I somehow missed mentioning him, and that's something I deeply regret. Because no retelling of my school journey is complete without him. He was there at the beginning. He remained through the years. And even now, he walks beside me, this time, as a mentor to my kids.

So thank you, Kamal Sir. For everything. For being there. For believing in me before I believed in myself. And for continuing to be part of our lives in the most beautiful, consistent way possible.

One of the biggest responsibilities I held in school was being the class monitor, from Class 8 to Class 10. Not once was that challenged. I was the monitor for three consecutive years, without a single contest. No elections, no discussions. It just continued. And one year, they even created an award just to recognize that consistency. I was proud of that. It felt like the school acknowledged not just my behavior, but the consistency of it. I wasn't the loudest voice in the room, but I was reliable.

I remember a friend once told me, "Vivek, you are like Wemmick." It was a character from *Great Expectations*, a book we were reading in our syllabus. Wemmick was known for having two personalities; he was strict and serious at work but jovial and fun at home. That comparison stayed with me. I think my friend Gaurav saw both sides of me. In school, I was all about discipline and studies. But outside, with friends or at home, I enjoyed myself, cracked jokes, and was more relaxed. That duality has remained with me even now. Professionally, I'm serious. Personally, I know how to unwind and enjoy the moment.

Behind all of this, my mother played a pivotal role. She gave us a kind of freedom that's rare. She wanted us to explore every opportunity, whether it was sports, cultural events, or anything new that came our way. She encouraged participation and openness. I never feared telling her anything, no matter how small or big. That bond of transparency was beautiful. And it wasn't just me. My sister also shared the same kind of open relationship with her. We would both come back from school, and one of the first things we'd do was sit with her and talk about our day.

That space to express, without fear or judgment, shaped my emotional confidence. It's why even today, I value open dialogue, both at home and in professional life. The foundation for that was laid back then, through small conversations at the dinner table, during walks, or late-night chats with my mother. She never imposed, only guided.

So when I look back, that phase from Class 8 to 10, under Ms. Thomas's guidance, under Abishai Sir's leadership, and supported unconditionally at home, was deeply formative. It wasn't about just academic growth. It was the shaping of character, principles, and confidence that still carry me through life.

Every evening, without fail, there would be a moment when I would sit with my mother. It didn't need to be a planned conversation or an elaborate talk. It could be while she was peeling vegetables in the kitchen or folding clothes, and I would just start sharing my day. What I said didn't matter as much as the fact that she always listened, deeply, patiently, and without interruption. She had this rare quality of being completely present. Her eyes would be calm, her hands still, and her expression never gave away what she might have been thinking.

She hardly reacted, never jumped in, never scolded midway, never laughed at something I was serious about. She waited. And when she felt that something required a response, she gave it, not more, not less. Just enough for me to think clearly. Her restraint taught me something I didn't realize back then: the strength in silence, the power in thoughtful responses over emotional reactions.

But whenever she felt I was about to cross a line, whether in tone, in intent, or in decision, she drew a clear boundary. Calmly, firmly, without raising her voice. "Don't ever do this," she would say. That was it. No long explanation, no sermon. Just a line drawn in sand that I knew not to step over. It wasn't fear that kept me from crossing it; it was respect. Her boundaries never felt like restrictions. They were spaces carved out for safety and understanding.

Over time, those moments with her became a silent classroom. Not of books and exams, but of life itself. Occasionally, she would open up about certain things in the family, situations, or stories that we had never heard about. We belonged to a large family, and like any large family, there were layers of unspoken histories, undercurrents of conflict, and decisions made in the past that shaped the present.

She never gossiped, never dramatized. She shared only what she thought would help us understand relationships better. Sometimes it was a subtle lesson: how a sibling bond can be fractured by ego, or how misunderstandings over property or money can scar generations. At other times, it was about emotions, jealousy, neglect, love, betrayal, all the things that make human relations so complicated.

Looking back, I realize how purposeful those stories were. She didn't want us to be shocked by life when it happened to us. She wanted us to be prepared, to know that the world was not black and white. Those relationships require effort, communication, and maturity. That love is not enough; understanding, patience, and forgiveness matter more.

She was raising not just obedient children, but emotionally intelligent human beings.

The way she taught us to handle our emotions shaped our personalities. She never told us to "not cry" or "be strong" in that stereotypical way. But by watching her be so balanced, so steady, we learned the difference between reacting and responding. We learned that maturity isn't about having all the answers; it's about asking the right questions and knowing when not to speak.

These weren't textbook lessons. They were living examples. And that was the beauty of it.

I think this is what made both my sister and me grow up a little earlier than others. Our maturity wasn't forced; it was cultivated naturally, quietly, through the culture of openness and trust at home. And that's also where, I believe, my seriousness came from. People often say I was too serious for my age, even back then. But it wasn't because I was burdened or sad. It was just the way I processed life, methodically, carefully, and with thought.

Even in school, this reflected in how I behaved. I wasn't playful in the traditional sense. I didn't enjoy pranks or casual gossip. But I loved solving things, helping people out, and staying focused on what mattered. I wasn't the loudest voice in a group, but if someone had a real problem, they would come to me.

I remember once, during our school's annual function preparations, there was a lot of chaos in our class about who would participate in what. Groups were forming, arguments were breaking out, and everyone seemed to have something to say. I sat silently for a long time, listening. And then, when no one else could bring the group together, I simply asked, "Can we write down everyone's name and interests on the board and see where they fit best?"

That calmed the room. We found a way to divide the work, and everyone got a role they were happy with. That was it. No drama, no speech. Just order through logic.

Later that day, Ms. Thomas called me aside and said, "You have an old soul, Vivek. You don't speak much, but you listen well. Don't lose that." That stayed with me.

Listening, something I inherited from my mother, became my strength. And when I say listening, I don't mean just hearing words. I mean understanding the silence behind them, the pauses that carry more meaning than the sentences, the emotions between the lines.

At home, this created a quiet balance. My sister and I, though different in our ways, shared that openness. We never feared telling our mother anything, not even our mistakes. We knew she wouldn't explode or dismiss us. That allowed us to be honest. Completely honest.

There were days when we came back from school upset, maybe someone teased us, or we didn't do well on a test. And there were other days filled with joy, when we won something or had fun with friends. No matter what it was, our first instinct was to tell

Mom. She would either smile knowingly or nod with understanding, or just say, “It’s okay. Try again tomorrow.”

That phrase, “Try again tomorrow”, carried hope. It meant the day wasn’t the end. There was always another chance.

In a world where children often hide things from their parents, this culture of openness was our emotional safety net. It built trust not just between us and her, but also within ourselves. We trusted our own thoughts more. We didn’t second-guess our instincts. And that kind of self-assurance comes only when you grow up in an environment where your voice is heard without judgment.

Of course, we weren’t perfect children. We made mistakes, argued with each other, and occasionally broke the rules. But the correction at home was never about punishment; it was always about understanding why something was wrong. That distinction is important. It didn’t make us feel small; it made us want to do better.

Over time, these values became the foundation of how I approached people and situations even outside of home. In college, at work, and in friendships, I carried that sense of calm, seriousness, and reflection. People sometimes found me difficult to read, but I wasn’t hiding anything. I was just taking time to understand before reacting.

And now, when I look at the person I’ve become, the way I handle crises, the way I deal with complex people or emotions, I know that so much of it goes back to those small daily conversations with my mother. No formal lessons, no manuals. Just presence, patience, and an unwavering belief in us.

She never told us to be successful. She told us to be sincere. She never pushed us to be the best; she asked us to be kind, to be responsible, and to be honest. Those words still ring in my head.

Even today, I find myself repeating them to others, colleagues, friends, younger cousins, and even to myself when I'm in doubt. That voice, her voice, is part of my inner compass.

And if I ever do become someone worthy of being remembered, I know it will be because of the foundation she laid. Quietly, patiently, and with great love.

Class 10 was a turning point for me, perhaps the first true test of my abilities, my motivation, and my sense of identity. I had always been a reasonably good student, quiet, disciplined, methodical, but until then, I hadn't really experienced failure in the academic sense. The pre-boards, however, were a rude awakening.

Maths had always been my stronghold. Numbers came naturally to me, formulas, patterns, logic, they all felt like a puzzle waiting to be solved. Even physics, which many students found intimidating, felt manageable because of the underlying logic and consistency. Chemistry was a mixed bag. Physical chemistry made sense, but organic chemistry and the rote memorization that came with it felt like an uphill climb. Still, I could manage.

But history and geography? That was a different world altogether.

No matter how many times I tried, I couldn't get myself to memorize those long, elaborate descriptions of battles, dates, or natural formations. I'd sit with the book open in front of me, my mind wandering, trying to create a story out of dry timelines and paragraphs filled with unfamiliar names. But it never stuck. My brain just wasn't built for cramming disconnected facts, and I had no technique to make the material mine.

So, when I got the pre-board results back, I was stunned. Geography, just pass marks. The red line was dangerously close. It was the first time in my life I had seen such a low score. I remember staring at the paper in disbelief, the numbers almost mocking me. I had never seen red ink on my mark sheet. It shook me. The feeling wasn't just of shame or fear; it was of disappointment in myself. If this was how I had performed in the pre-boards, what would happen in the actual Class 10 boards?

People had expectations: my teachers, my parents, even my classmates. They all assumed I would do well. Somewhere, I had also started believing in that image. The idea of not living up to that faith was unbearable. That one mark sheet became a wake-up call. It was like someone had splashed cold water on my face. The stakes were real now. And I realized I had a choice: either accept mediocrity or fight back.

And so, I decided to fight.

I made a plan. I divided my day, I blocked time for each subject, and I focused on the weak spots. But there was one subject that continued to challenge me more than others: biology. I knew I couldn't afford to stumble there, not again. And this time, I didn't hesitate to ask for help.

I went to my father and told him honestly, "Biology is not working out. I need help." He didn't question me or ask why I hadn't done well before. Instead, he acted immediately. He called one of his friends, a doctor, and explained the situation.

That doctor introduced me to a teacher, someone I met just once. Yes, just once. For 16 minutes.

I remember the date vividly. It was the 21st. We met in a small room with a whiteboard and a single chair. I don't even remember his name now, but I will never forget what he taught me in those precious 16 minutes. He didn't dive into the chapters or throw jargon at me. Instead, he asked me a simple question: "Do you understand how your own body works?"

I shook my head.

He smiled and said, "That's where you begin. Biology is not about books. It's about *you*. Your body. Your systems. Your reactions. Don't learn biology like a textbook. Learn it like you're learning your own story."

And then he began explaining how every chapter in biology could be linked to something I could feel, see, or experience. Heartbeats, digestion, breathing, movement, immunity, each topic could be mapped onto something real, something personal. He showed me how to use association, how to visualize organs, systems, and cells, and how to create mind maps that didn't just dump information, but connected ideas.

Those 16 minutes were a revolution.

For the first time, biology made sense. It wasn't a monster anymore. It was my own body talking to me. After that day, I stopped dreading the subject. I began looking at diagrams not as forced sketches but as blueprints of life. I made charts. I spoke things out loud. I practiced active recall. And most importantly, I began enjoying the process.

This new approach extended to other subjects as well. Geography became easier when I began looking at maps as stories of the Earth's journey. History became manageable when I created timelines that linked events to causes and consequences, rather than memorizing random dates.

I didn't have a tutor, nor did I attend any coaching. I just learned how to learn. And that, more than anything else, changed the game.

As the board exams approached, I felt more prepared than ever before. I wasn't overconfident, but I was steady. I had put in the work, day by day, hour by hour, staying up late some nights, waking early on others. There were moments of doubt, moments when I felt the weight of expectations again. But I kept reminding myself, it's okay to fail once. It's not okay to quit trying.

When the results came, I remember logging in with shaking fingers. The number that flashed on the screen brought relief first, then joy, and finally, a quiet sense of pride. Over 80%. Distinction.

Not a top rank. Not a record-breaking score. But it was mine. Earned, fought for, and meaningful.

Everyone at home celebrated. My father was proud, my mother hugged me and said something that has stayed with me ever since: "This is not just about marks. This is about learning how to overcome fear."

And that was the truth.

What Class 10 taught me wasn't just syllabus material. It taught me life material. That failure is a sign, not a verdict. That asking for help isn't a weakness; it's wisdom. That even a 16-minute conversation can alter your direction. That discipline, when combined with the right strategy, can move mountains.

It also taught me something deeper: that self-belief is a muscle. You have to build it, one small win at a time. And sometimes, the most important victories are the ones you have over your own doubts.

When school reopened after the boards, and we began our journey into Class 11, people treated me a little differently. Some were surprised by my scores. Others expected I would now aim for IIT or a medical college. But for me, the destination didn't matter as much as the mindset I had acquired.

That seriousness, which people had always commented on, had now become purpose. I wasn't just the boy who spoke less. I was someone who knew how to quietly transform a weakness into a strength. That identity became my quiet badge of honor.

Over the years, that 10th-grade experience has acted like a reference point. Whenever life threw a challenge my way, be it in academics, relationships, or later, in my professional career, I remembered that time. That one geography mark sheet. That biology session. That long period of late nights and silent discipline.

It reminds me even today that if I could face my worst subject and still come out strong, there's nothing I can't face.

And perhaps that's the real lesson: The biggest exams in life don't come with hall tickets or invigilators. They come quietly, disguised as disappointments. And how we respond to them defines who we are.

The result of my Class 10 board exams had not just given me a certificate or a score, but it had given me confidence. A kind of quiet, unshakeable belief that I could shape my own outcomes. That if I gave my best, input after input, without obsessing over results, the outcome would take care of itself. That belief, which had first taken root during the pre-board struggle, began to grow stronger inside me.

It was a mental shift. A personal realization. I wasn't someone who relied on luck or comparisons anymore. I had tasted the power of hard work, of seeking help when needed, and of finding new ways to learn. I had become someone who could *trust himself*. And that trust became the bedrock of everything that followed.

After Class 10, most students in my school were faced with a major decision: whether to stay in Begusarai for Classes 11 and 12 or to move out to bigger cities for better exposure, more coaching, and more "serious" career preparation. Patna, Ranchi, and Delhi were the destinations everyone seemed to be considering. Some had already enrolled in coaching institutes. Others had relatives who offered to take them in.

It was a time of transition. Everyone was moving in different directions, and for a brief moment, I was caught in that dilemma too.

But deep down, my heart had already made a decision. I wanted to stay. Stay in Begusarai. Stay in St. Paul's. Stay with the familiar faces and the familiar walls that had shaped me for so many years. And, more than anything, stay under the watchful, encouraging presence of *Sarama Jannet Thomas.*

Ms. Thomas had become more than a teacher to me. She was an anchor. A figure of immense stability, calm, and quiet discipline. For years, I had seen her guiding not just me but many others, but I always felt there was something special in the bond we shared. She saw potential in me, and more importantly, she trusted my intent. And that meant a lot.

While other students complained about her being too strict, I always saw the method behind her discipline. Her rules weren't random; they were values in disguise. I admired her firmness, her sense of order, and her silent affection toward those who respected that order. I knew if I stayed, she would be around. And knowing she was there, someone who understood me, who cared, felt deeply comforting.

In some ways, I've always been a homely person. Soft at heart. Attached to my roots. I was never the sort of boy who could just pack a bag and start life in a hostel or a new city without a second thought. I needed warmth. Familiarity. Trust. I needed to feel safe.

And Begusarai, at that time, still gave me all of that.

There's also something about the emotional rhythms of home that cannot be easily replaced. The sound of my mother's voice, the quiet corners where I used to study, the comforting clatter of utensils from the kitchen during evening tea-time, all these formed a cocoon I wasn't ready to leave. Not yet.

My mother, too, had an unspoken wish. She never pushed it on me, but I knew. She wanted me to stay until Class 12. She believed I needed more time, time to grow emotionally, mentally, and perhaps even spiritually, before I stepped out into the world. And she wasn't wrong.

At that stage, I still didn't have a full understanding of what "career" meant. The word itself felt abstract, something distant and complex. Engineering, medical, UPSC, chartered accountancy, these were terms floating around in conversations, but none of them had sunk in deeply enough for me to shape a path. My focus was simpler: continue what I had started, build on my momentum, and grow as a student and a person.

I had no roadmap, but I had direction.

And so, while many of my classmates moved to bigger cities, enrolled in top-tier institutes, and began preparing for competitive exams, I made a different choice. I stayed back. I stayed in St. Paul's.

It wasn't an easy decision. There were moments of doubt, especially when relatives or neighbors would ask, "Why aren't you going outside? You should be in Patna or Kota now." There was always an undertone of judgment in such questions, as if staying in Begusarai was somehow a compromise. But I didn't see it that way.

For me, staying was not about fear or comfort; it was about building myself step by step. I wasn't in a race with anyone. I had learned that from my 10th board experience. I was only in competition with my past self.

The next two years, in Class 11 and 12, were deeply formative.

I chose the science stream, naturally. Maths, Physics, Chemistry, and English. I immersed myself in my subjects. I carried forward the same discipline and intensity that I had developed in Class 10. My methods improved. I became more analytical, more curious. I wasn't just studying to score; I was studying to understand.

But these years weren't just about academics. They were also about subtle emotional growth. I became more aware of people, of relationships, of myself. I understood what kind of environment nurtured me. I noticed how discipline, when internalized, becomes freedom. I noticed how support systems, like that of my teachers, especially Ms. Thomas, could quietly transform a child's self-image.

It was also during this time that I began developing a better sense of independence, without ever having to leave home. I started making my own decisions about how to study, when to rest, whom to seek guidance from, and how to use my time. There was a new confidence in my daily life.

And slowly, a new word began to enter my vocabulary: *ambition*.

I didn't yet know what exact profession I would pursue. But I knew I wanted to go beyond the borders of Begusarai one day. I wanted to see more of the world, understand how systems work, how leadership functions, and how organizations are built. I had a growing interest in people and ideas. And I knew that when the time came, I would be ready.

The foundation was being laid in classrooms filled with chalk dust and soft-spoken teachers, in the quiet hours spent with textbooks, and in the everyday interactions with my family, which continued to be a source of strength.

My mother, as always, remained my emotional anchor. She never interfered in my studies, never pressured me about marks or choices. But she was always there, listening, supporting, and encouraging. She had a rare ability to guide without imposing. And I think that allowed me to mature naturally.

She trusted me. And because she trusted me, I learned to trust myself.

Looking back, those two years in Begusarai weren't just an extension of school. They were the final layers of my childhood. They helped me make peace with who I was and gave me the clarity to imagine who I could become.

Many people think that growth only happens when you break away from your past, when you leave home, or step into a new city. But sometimes, staying in one place can offer you something even deeper, a grounding, a sense of self, a clarity of values.

That's what St. Paul's and Begusarai gave me.

And Ms. Thomas remained a constant. A quiet supporter. A mentor. I still remember the small smiles she gave when I did well in class, the rare words of appreciation, the occasional warning when I got too relaxed. She never micromanaged, but she was always aware. Her presence reminded me that excellence is often a habit, not an act.

By the time Class 12 ended, I was no longer the unsure boy who had struggled with geography and biology. I was someone who had begun to shape his own mind. I wasn't just preparing for exams anymore; I was preparing for life.

Chapter 3: Stepping into Engineering Without a Background in Computers

Class 11 was a quiet revolution in my academic life, not due to the syllabus, not even due to the coming-of-age sensation that is said to accompany the "senior" classes, but simply because I had at last shed biology.

Yes, for me, it was freedom from biology. That single subject had always been on my mind, not because I disliked studying, but because I didn't enjoy mugging up on what didn't relate. I required logic, application, and a pattern. Biology, with its endless diagrams and mechanical memorization, provided none of those. The day I entered Class 11 and realized I would no longer have to struggle through it, a tremendous burden was lifted off my shoulders.

Now I was able to concentrate on topics that made my head feel alive: math, physics, and chemistry. Organic chemistry, of course, still posed its problems. Reactions, conversions, and mechanisms, these weren't a piece of cake, but at least I could handle them. At least now, the underpinnings of my coursework were consistent with the way I thought, the way I operated in the world.

I had to study Hindi as my second language. It was a strategic decision; English and Hindi were two languages I knew I could do, and I did not want any undue strain pulling down my performance in the board exams. If anything, I wanted subjects that boosted my confidence, that allowed me to express my actual capability without pretending to be interested. Hindi, I was sure, would be a break in the midst of the tempest of formulas and equations.

It was also during this period that I encountered someone who would define my path more deeply than I then knew, Professor George.

He was our instructor in physics and math. He was from the same Green House as me, not a real greenhouse, obviously, but one of the four house systems St. Paul's used. I'd always been in the Green House, and he was its head. So there was already this strange feeling of connection, a familiarity prior even to the first class. But when the sessions commenced, it wasn't long before he realised that I had a knack for numbers.

He was not a dramatic kind of teacher. He didn't storm in class or hurl chalk like we had seen in Bollywood films. He was calm, steady, and perceptive, and what differentiated him was that he looked at students. Actually, saw them. Their potential, their deficits, their speed, their fire. He saw that in me. He saw my hold on mathematics and physics. And the dearest thing he gave me was not marks or medals, but something much more enduring, confidence.

He believed in me. Truly.

It's interesting how another person's belief in you can alter how you view yourself. When you respect someone and you think that they believe in you, it doesn't feel nice; it reconfigures your mind. With Professor George, I began challenging myself further. Not because I feared getting punished, but because I wanted to justify the faith he had in me. I wanted to make his trust worth it.

I still recall a specific moment in Class 12. It was either the pre-board or the internal exam, I am not sure, but my memory is fresh. He was going through my maths paper in front of me, page after page, flipping through, marking each answer with such reassuring surety.

Tick. Tick. Tick. Tick.

I cannot believe it. I was nervous and excited at the same time. No hesitation. He just continued going, believing my answers. And deep down in me, my heart filled up. This was not an examination; it was an indication of the amount of faith he had in my work. I felt proud. I felt appreciated.

Later, however, I read through the paper myself, and I realized something, a blunder. A little calculation error. He had overlooked it in the momentum.

Most of the students would have just left it at that. I mean, who in their right mind would volunteer to lose marks? But I couldn't. Something within me wouldn't allow it. So I approached him and I highlighted it.

And that small incident altered something within me forever.

He corrected the mark with grace, smiled, and said something I'll never forget. He said, "When students show this kind of honesty, it reflects more than just good values; it reflects that they've become true learners."

That sentence stayed with me. That moment became a compass. It taught me that it's not just about being right, it's about being trustworthy. That your work, your output, and your behaviour should inspire confidence in people around you. That trust, once earned, is the most powerful currency in life.

From there on, "doing quality work" wasn't only about right answers. It was doing things so that people could trust you with their eyes closed. It was about establishing a reputation, not a résumé.

That attitude, which Professor George inadvertently facilitated in me, came to be one of the foundations of my working life. When I began leading groups, working with people, and making decisions, I saw how important trust is to accomplishing anything. You can't control everything by micromanaging. You need folks you can trust, and you need to be someone who's worthy of being trusted.

Back at school, though, I didn't know all this yet. I only knew that something within me had changed. I no longer studied for the sake of scoring. I was constructing myself.

And that construction process was yielding dividends.

When Class 12 results were announced, it was a dreamy kind of moment. I had achieved 88%, a figure that was thrilling and also humbling. For someone who barely passed geography at pre-boards in Class 10, this was a giant step. But more than the figure, it was what it meant.

It was a reinforcement of everything I had started to believe in: that consistent effort matters more than overnight success. That staying back in Begusarai, in my familiar school, under teachers who cared, not just about curriculum but about character, had been the right choice. That trusting my instincts, focusing on inputs, and staying honest to my process had led to the best output of all, self-belief.

I had topped the school that year. Something I had never even imagined. I, the shy boy from Green House, who had once doubted his own abilities, am now a school topper. It was intimidating. But it was also humbling. For I knew what had led me there.

Commitment. Dedication. Inputs.

There were no shortcuts, no eleventh-hour revelations. There was only consistent focus, a community of trust among teachers, and the conviction that good work, when created with authenticity, would always be recognized.

And as I stood there clutching my mark sheet that day, something else began to take hold of me in silence. A new chapter was about to be opened. One where I was going to leave behind the comfort of home, the protective eye of teachers like Professor George, and venture into an unknown realm, engineering.

A world I didn't even know much about yet. A world of coding, computers, and machines, and I didn't even have a computer background.

When I walked out of St. Paul's with my Class 12 results in hand, there was a quiet sense of achievement in me, but not celebration. To me, results were not about showing the world anything. Honestly, I didn't even know what these marks would eventually mean. I didn't know what it meant to have a career or how exactly good grades would lead to anything concrete in life.

What I did know, and very deeply believed in, was that this was my duty. Studying was my job. I was always told that this was my karma, my form of puja. There was never a conversation around what package I'll get, what position I'll be in, or anything of that sort. It was simple. "This is what you have to do now, and you must do it well."

So I did.

And then came the next step, engineering.

Now, when I say I didn't have a background in computers, I mean in a formal sense. True, we never had formal computer classes in school. But I wouldn't say computers were completely alien to me either. When we moved from Kolkata to Begusarai in 1995, my grandfather made a sincere effort to make sure I didn't feel that shift as a downgrade. He introduced things to our home that could help me stay interested, engaged, and one of those things was a desktop computer.

It was a massive deal in those days. Not many households had computers, and here I was, a boy in Begusarai with a full desktop setup. My grandfather also arranged for Kamal Sir, a young teacher who introduced me to the world of computing at a very basic level, how to turn it on, how to use Paint, MS Word, DOS commands, and such things. I didn't know programming. But yes, computers weren't a mystery to me. I could navigate them. And that gave me a quiet confidence when I took up Computer Science in engineering.

There was no fear. There was no voice in my head saying, You won't be able to do this. I had already decided. I knew I wanted to do this. And for me, when something becomes a decision, I don't look for validation or fear rejection; I just get into it.

But the real challenge didn't come from the subject. It came from people.

You see, every class has a core group, the ones who know a bit more, who are more confident, more vocal, often more experienced. And in my engineering batch, there was this group of 10 to 12 students who already had a strong grasp of computers. Some had done courses from NIIT or Aptech. Some had done projects in C++ or Java in school. So naturally, they were ahead. But more importantly, they knew they were ahead, and they formed their own group.

Initially, I didn't think much of it. Everyone has their comfort circles. But then came the group project assignment: a chatbot. It was a big deal back then in 2003. Chatbots weren't as mainstream as they are now, and this was an ambitious project. So, naturally, all eyes were on that core group to lead the way.

I wasn't included.

At first, I thought it was an oversight. I waited. But no invitation came. It wasn't even a polite, "Hey, we're full, but let's do something together later." Nothing. I only came to know that I wasn't part of the group through my teacher, not even from the friends I thought I had made.

And I was shattered.

Not because I wasn't chosen. But because of how it happened, without a word, without any conversation. That silent exclusion, done behind my back, hurt in a way I had never experienced before. It felt like betrayal. And at that age, in a new city, surrounded by unfamiliar faces and overwhelming coursework, this one act felt like the entire ground beneath me had shifted.

I remember calling home in tears. Just tears, no words. My mother immediately sensed that something was wrong. She came to Delhi the very next day. I don't know how she did it, leaving everything, traveling overnight, but she came and met me and then met my teacher.

And what my teacher told her changed everything for me.

She said something so simple, yet so profound. "What difference does it make if someone knows things beforehand? He just has to study what's in the syllabus. The same syllabus that will come in the exam. That's all that matters."

That logic hit me like a bolt of lightning.

It was so clear, so rational, and yet I hadn't seen it. I was too caught up in emotions. Too shaken by exclusion. But my teacher's words gave me perspective. It wasn't about what others knew; it was about what I was willing to learn. The syllabus was the same for everyone. No one had an unfair advantage in the actual exam. All I had to do was stick to the plan, put in the work, and not get distracted by noise.

That became my mantra. And I stayed.

I didn't leave. I didn't sulk. I didn't try to win over the core group. I moved forward.

I formed a new group. Not the smartest in the class, not the loudest, not the ones who knew everything. But good people. Sincere people. 4 or 5 of them. We weren't close friends then, but we shared a common purpose: to learn. And I took it upon myself to lead that learning.

If there were a presentation, I would go deeper than anyone else. If there was a topic to be explained, I would take responsibility to understand it inside out. I began studying for understanding, not just grades. Because I knew that the real test wasn't marks, it was standing in front of those 10 students and answering their questions.

And that was my new fear.

Not the subject. Not the content. But the audience. Those 10 students. Every time I had to present something, I knew they would be in front, arms crossed, eyes judging, waiting to ask difficult questions. They weren't being cruel. But I knew they didn't believe in me. And the only way to change that was to be unshakable in what I was saying.

So I studied.

Not superficially. I studied deeply. I anticipated every possible question. I cross-verified every code line. I rehearsed every explanation. Because that fear, that fear of being seen as "less than", was not going to win.

And slowly, something magical began to happen.

I started gaining confidence, not from external approval, but from internal clarity. I began to realize that understanding something deeply gives you a strength that no amount of prior experience can give. You don't need to be the first to the race. You just need to finish strong.

The same people who had once ignored me now began to acknowledge my effort. The teachers noticed my presentations, my dedication. My group started trusting me blindly. I had earned something priceless, not sympathy, but respect.

Looking back now, I realize how defining that phase was. It could have broken me. It could have made me bitter or withdrawn. But instead, it gave me a mindset I've carried ever since: If you're not invited to the table, build your own table. And make it stronger.

It also gave me clarity about the nature of knowledge. Every subject is unfamiliar when you begin. Everything worth learning looks difficult at first. But the difference is made not by what you already know, but by what you're willing to endure to understand it.

That keyboard project? I didn't just contribute to it, I owned it. I understood it better than those who had sidelined me. I explained the entire working of the keyboard, deeply. And in that small classroom, where lines of C++ floated in the air like a second language, I gave my first real presentation in the world of computers, not as a novice, but as a self-made learner.

That was the beginning.

The beginning of my trusting myself more than the opinions of others. The beginning of my realizing that effort levels the playing field. And the beginning of a lifelong relationship with challenges, where I no longer feared them but welcomed them.

Because from that point forward, I knew one thing with certainty:

There is no such thing as an unfamiliar subject, only unfamiliar effort.

If there was one turning point that helped me cross the bridge from fear to confidence in my early engineering days, it was that first group project with my new set of teammates. I remember it so vividly, almost like it happened yesterday. The topic was simple on the surface: How does a keyboard work? But for me, it was a doorway into a new world.

I took the assignment seriously. I don't remember exactly where I gathered the material from, probably a mix of books, a couple of library resources, and the early internet. But I do remember spending days trying to understand the actual logic behind how pressing a key translates to something appearing on the screen. I wasn't just mugging up lines from a textbook; I was going deep into circuitry, interrupt requests, scan codes, and everything else that made a keyboard tick.

I worked with my new group, those four or five people who had agreed to team up with me, and I didn't hold back. I shared everything I had learnt with them. I made diagrams, explained concepts, and cross-checked their slides, and in that process, something changed.

When we gave that presentation, it went far better than I had imagined. The teacher appreciated our effort, and for the first time, I didn't just feel like I had completed a task; I felt validated. Not by others, but by myself. Because I had taken a topic I had zero prior knowledge about, and I had made it my own. That moment planted a seed. A seed of resilience. A seed of self-belief.

It told me: You don't need to be a part of the "cool" group to succeed.

You just need to do the work. Consistently. Deeply. And with curiosity.

And the most satisfying part? During that presentation, the so-called experts from the original group, yes, the very people who had once excluded me, couldn't ask a single question. Not because they didn't want to. But because they had nothing to question. Everything I presented was rock-solid. That silence from them was louder than applause. That was a moment of quiet victory. And it set the tone for the next four years.

In my first year of engineering, I didn't top the class. I got 81%. The person who had played a key role in forming the earlier clique scored around 85–86%. So yes, he was still ahead numerically. But in terms of effort, learning, and mindset, I had taken a huge leap.

Because for the first time, I had truly become independent in learning. I wasn't just absorbing what others told me. I was seeking. I was exploring. I had learnt something priceless: You don't need someone else to teach you everything. You just need good sources and a strong intent. That's it.

And that became my compass.

Every time I sat with a new topic, I didn't skim through it. I didn't aim for "just enough to pass." I went deep. Because the world doesn't reward half-efforts. If you want to win, you have to go deep. Go deep enough to find answers nobody else is willing to look for.

This wasn't something I did because I wanted praise or marks. I did it because it made me feel alive. Learning became my source of joy. It wasn't a chore anymore. It was a choice. And this kept me going, even when the road became even more uncertain.

Which brings me to another challenge, a massive one.

Sometime during our third semester, the college received a piece of devastating news. The university affiliation was cancelled. We were suddenly in limbo. Imagine working hard, believing that you're on a path to a degree, and then hearing that your college is no longer recognized. It felt like the floor had been pulled out from under us. No one knew what would happen next. Classes were still running, but technically, we had no university to award us degrees.

It was a confusing time. Fear crept in. Doubts started to multiply. Would we graduate? Would we get jobs? Was all this effort for nothing?

In that chaos, something unusual happened. Instead of feeling defeated, a strange idea started taking root in me: Maybe this is the time to learn something different.

I can't tell you exactly where the idea came from. Maybe it was the confidence I had started to develop after that first project. Maybe it was the sense of rebellion I carried against the traditional route that had already excluded me once. But whatever it was, I found myself thinking: Why should I only learn what everyone else is learning?

I wanted to explore beyond the prescribed curriculum.

That's when I discovered Red Hat Certified Engineer (RHCE). A specialized course in Linux and server management. Nobody in my class was doing it. It wasn't something you would take up unless you were genuinely interested in how networks and systems worked.

I asked around, some friends, some classmates, if they'd want to join. No one seemed keen. And honestly, they didn't discourage me. But they didn't encourage me either. It was more like a polite nod that said, Okay, you do your thing.

And I did.

I didn't complete the certification officially because I never sat for the final exam. But I did the entire course. Every class. Every module. I did it diligently. I experimented. I built mock server systems. I configured networks. I worked with virtual machines. And somewhere along the way, the blurry concepts of "internet," "server," and "backend systems" started becoming crystal clear to me.

What that course gave me was far beyond the syllabus. It gave me a foundation in real-world computer science. It connected the dots between what we studied and how it actually applied. I could now visualize how a request travels through a network, how a server responds, how load balancing works, and how systems crash and recover.

It made everything else easier to understand.

But more than that, it gave me something to hold on to during uncertain times. When our college's future was unclear, when my peers were confused or demotivated, I had this one thing that kept me going: my learning. I knew I was becoming better. Whether or not I got a degree, whether or not someone recognized it, I was gaining knowledge that no one could take away from me.

And that was a game-changer.

By the time we reached the end of our fourth semester, I had grown in ways I couldn't have imagined. I was no longer trying to prove myself to anyone. I was just learning, every single day, because I loved it. That love became my fuel. It still is.

Over time, I started topping classes. Slowly, gradually. Not with pressure, but with peace. Because I had discovered the secret: when you fall in love with the process, the results follow. They have to.

Also, much later in life, I took the CliftonStrengths assessment. If you're familiar with it, you'd know it identifies your core strengths based on your patterns of behavior and thinking. The top strength that came out for me?

Learner.

No surprise.

Because I had seen it manifest, years ago, right there in that college classroom, through those books, projects, setbacks, and late nights. I had become a learner in the purest sense. Not someone who studied for grades. But someone who studied because it was his way of engaging with the world.

That quality, of learning deeply and consistently, has stayed with me through every career shift, every challenge, every new domain I've entered. And I can trace its origins to those early years. To that keyboard project. To that RHCE course. To those rejections. To those moments when I could have quit, but chose to learn instead.

In retrospect, I believe all these things, each rejection, each solitary attempt, each achievement won through hard work, contributed to forging a profound change in how I perceived myself and the world around me. Gradually, steadily, I was maturing, not merely emotionally, but in how I learned and lived. My outlook was shifting. I was no longer a person who required a group, a peer group, or validation to proceed. I had started to take for myself a very simple but potent fact: this journey is mine, and I must walk it by myself if necessary.

I've mentioned before, but it bears repeating, study was my devotion. It was the one thing I knew for sure. While others who surrounded me did things differently to express themselves or pursue their passions, some enjoyed debating, some played sports, others socialized or partook in college fests, I had this one quiet, consistent thing that grounded me: studying.

And I don't mean memorizing textbooks or copying down assignments for the deadline. I mean actual study, the type that gets under your skin, where time flies and you don't even notice. You block out the noise around you because you're in the zone of getting something done. That was my domain. That was my universe. That was my shrine.

And maybe it was advantageous that I was introverted by nature. I didn't crave going out to parties or lingering about idly. I was a homebody, happy with books, quiet rooms, and thoughts that curled inward. There was no FOMO. Just a quiet voice in my head: "This is your way. Continue."

I believe that harmony between my character and my adopted discipline was a blessing. I didn't know it was what it was then, but I do now. Because that introspective focus, that self-discipline of reading deeply and persistently, had become who I was. And it had become the fuel that propelled me to the top of my college, not just once, but repeatedly. But more than that, it instilled in me confidence. A quiet, unshakeable kind. The kind that doesn't require validation.

The lessons of those times were straightforward, but they've lasted with me throughout my life.

First: don't rely on others.

Yes, we are in a society, and cooperation is vital. But if we are growing, particularly mentally growing, there are certain paths that need to be walked alone. You cannot always rely on someone to sit with you, to teach you, to prod you along. You have to make that engine within. And when you do, nobody can stop you.

Second: effort is more than anything else.

It's not about natural ability or who knows what prior. The individual who tries harder, who digs deeper, who perseveres, that's the individual who ultimately wins. I witnessed this repeatedly throughout my college years. The individuals who began as stars because they knew more initially? Some of them plateaued. And the ones that continued learning? They ascended. Quietly. Consistently. And remained on top.

Third: trust others, but carefully.

Not all will be your advocate. That's fine. But others will, and it can change everything. With me, it was my mother. Always. Her faith in me was never broken. And then there was my class teacher, a conversation she had with my mother, reassuring her not to worry because I simply needed to concentrate on the syllabus, which altered the course of my life. Sometimes, a single sentence, uttered at the precise moment by the correct person, is all you require.

So, yes, trust, but without blind faith. Trust those whose words embolden you. Trust those who illuminate, not muddle. Their advice can serve as a compass in moments of doubt about yourself.

Fourth: go deep, not wide.

I can't stress this enough. Depth is what it's all about. Surface knowledge will take you so far. True strength, true confidence, and true mastery all stem from depth. When you learn something in depth, when you know its why and how, you're not only studying for exams, you're studying for life. And this mindset, this determination to go deep, served me well to stand out from the pack.

Because in a class of 70 or 60, a lot will get the same marks. But hardly anyone will take it upon themselves to study something out of the syllabus. Hardly anyone will study because they enjoy doing it. I wanted to be among the handful.

That's why I opted for the RHCE course, Red Hat Certified Engineer. No one had requested me. It wasn't included in our normal curriculum. And it wasn't easy. But it was different. It challenged me. It instructed me on how servers functioned, how the internet worked at a level that no textbook had done up to then. I didn't take the final certification test, but I worked through each module, each lab. I played. I crashed systems. I repaired them. And along the way, I learned.

That class became one of the largest distinctions for me. It differentiated me, not just intellectually, but psychologically.

Because once you become accustomed to dealing with problems on your own, you cease to fear them.

And that brings me to one more learning: well begun is only half done.

Yes, it starts. Taking that initial step, making that first move, that's strong. But it's not sufficient. The true test is: can you be consistent? Can you keep pushing forward even when there is no ovation, no praise, no immediate payoff?

That's what I endeavored to do. I endeavored to keep that intensity till the very end. It wasn't always simple. There were distractions, there were doubts, there were temptations. But I kept reminding myself again and again: You started this journey for a reason. Complete it with the same sincerity.

And finally, I did. By the last year of engineering, I was no longer a student. I had become an independent self-starter. I no longer feared new subjects. I had given up asking someone to help me whenever I got stuck. I had developed a muscle, a learning muscle, that could haul me through anything.

And that's my biggest learning from all those years.

Because life doesn't end pushing you after you graduate from college. In fact, the true test begins thereafter. But if you've learned how to learn, deeply, autonomously, happily, then you possess a resilience that no circumstance can shatter.

Ultimately, I always return to that one sentence: study is my worship.

It was true back then. It's true today. Only the terms have widened. Now, "study" doesn't include just books. It includes understanding people, learning new things, and coping with change. But the essence remains the same. That silent space, that single-minded attention, that intense concentration, that's still where I am. That's still where I feel most at home.

So, to anyone reading this, or listening to this, or perhaps walking a similar path, this is what I would say:

You don't need to have all the answers today. You don't need to be part of the smartest group. You don't need to start ahead.

You just need to begin.

Begin with sincerity. With focus. With the willingness to go deep.

And then keep going.

Day by day. Book by book. Line by line.

That's how learners are made. That's how lives are changed.

Chapter 4: Dealing with Cancellation of College Affiliation

Now, coming to the college affiliation cancellation, my first reaction, I'm not exactly sure how I felt back then, but what I do remember is that I didn't quite understand the magnitude of it at first. The phrase "affiliation cancellation" sounded technical, almost bureaucratic. I did not know what it really meant. Well, I was merely a school boy, I went to classes, I had my homework, and I studied to take my in-school tests. To the best of my knowledge, it was still open in its classrooms, its teachers were still teaching, and I was still a student. I was broke, like most students in the department of engineering, trying to pay bills on a weekly basis, but other than that, I did not mind. The concept that something so structural, something invisible like affiliation, could derail my entire education hadn't sunk in.

The real implications started creeping in slowly, like whispers making their way through the corridors of the college. Some students began to murmur, "How will we get a degree now?" "Will companies even consider us for jobs without a proper university tag?" That's when it started dawning on me, bit by bit. It was not about whether the classes were going on or not. It was about the recognition, the validation that comes from a legitimate degree.

Of course, today, now that I'm in the corporate world, I completely understand what a degree stands for. Back then, I didn't. To me, education was a karmic act. As I've said before, studies were worship. That's all I knew. The idea that a piece of paper, your degree, could decide your credibility in the world? That was abstract for me then.

In those early days of the cancellation, the classes didn't stop immediately. They went on for a while, till the fifth semester, if I recall correctly. Students still turned up. Teachers still turned up. There was this collective hope, maybe even denial, that the issue would get resolved. There were talks, some kind of internal protests, a few trips to the university, but no clear answers. I was too busy with my own studies to pay much attention to the noise. For me, the logic was simple: if the classes are happening, then why panic?

But yes, after the fifth semester, things started unravelling. There were no more formal classes after that. I think it was sometime between the fifth and sixth semesters that reality started to settle in. There was restlessness in the air, panic even. People began planning their exit routes. Some were looking at transfer options. Others were planning to start over. That's when I started hearing things like, "Start preparing for CAT." And while I didn't know what lay ahead, I knew one thing: I couldn't afford to sit idle.

So, here's what I did. I decided I would study something parallel. If the main path was blocked or uncertain, I would carve a side path. This was the time I began my Red Hat Certified Engineer (RHCE) course. I mentioned this earlier; it was not a mainstream thing, not something our syllabus required. But it gave me direction. It gave me something to hold on to. The classes for that happened separately from college, and I poured myself into that completely.

One thing I can say with clarity is that this period taught me how to recalibrate. I didn't use that word back then. But that's what I was doing, shifting goals, adjusting expectations, and yet staying on course internally. Because deep down, the focus remained the same: learn, grow, move forward.

The big recalibration came when I realized that the engineering path may not conclude the way I had envisioned. So I told myself, Let's try something else. Let's prepare for CAT.

I still remember this clearly; it was January 2006. The classes had stopped. My engineering coursework was effectively paused. Fifth semester done, sixth semester uncertain, seventh and eighth semester nowhere in sight. And in that vacuum, I needed something to channel my energy into. I needed a goal.

MBA had always sounded fancy, though not necessarily "my" goal from the beginning. But it seemed like the right next step. It had structure. It had the possibility. And most importantly, it had certainty, a set syllabus, a set date, and a measurable outcome. So I enrolled in Career Launcher, one of the better-known CAT coaching institutes in Delhi. I told myself that even if the engineering degree doesn't come through the way I want, I'll prepare for an MBA, I'll give CAT, and that will be my next chapter.

And so began that intense year of preparation.

CAT prep isn't easy. It demands discipline, strategy, and a different kind of thinking. It's not just about what you know, but about how fast you can apply it. But for me, having always been self-motivated, it wasn't a challenge to sit and study for long hours. The challenge was managing the inner chaos, the questions that sometimes came up late at night: Will this even matter if my degree isn't valid? What if this MBA dream also collapses? What if I've wasted the last three years?

But every time those thoughts crept in, I reminded myself, This is your karma. Your job is to study, to prepare, to give your 100%. The rest will take care of itself. And somehow, that faith, that simplicity of thought, kept me grounded.

Career Launcher became my new classroom. I made new friends. I solved hundreds of mock questions. Quant, Verbal, Logical Reasoning, Data Interpretation, I immersed myself in all of it. I studied in libraries. I made flashcards. I challenged myself to beat my last mock test scores. And somewhere in all of that, the noise about the affiliation, the degree uncertainty, the halted semesters, it all faded into the background.

The classes for CAT went on for almost the whole year. Every week, I grew sharper. More confident. I understood my strengths. Quant was easy for me, Verbal not so much. But I worked on it. I practiced. Repeated. Improved.

November 2006 came. The CAT exam day.

I walked in feeling a mix of nervousness and calm. Nervous, because of what was at stake. Calm, because I knew I had prepared as well as I could. I think that is the peace you earn when you've truly given your best. The results, as always, would follow.

And that, in some way, marks the end of that phase. From affiliation cancellation to MBA preparation, what could have been a chaotic, lost year turned out to be one of my most focused, growth-oriented years. It taught me how to cope with uncertainty. How to find stability not in outcomes, but in action. How to keep walking even when the road ahead disappears.

And most importantly, it taught me how to recalibrate, not once, but as many times as life demands.

And I had to do the MBA. Least expected. What was going to happen next, I couldn't really say. I didn't even know if I was going to get a degree. What was going to happen in MBA, I had no clue. I hadn't planned this far ahead. The path I had walked so far had been more about walking sincerely than walking with a destination in mind. So when the college affiliation got canceled, I didn't even grasp its weight in the beginning. I only began to understand its seriousness slowly, like someone waking up from a light sleep into a storm.

What that whole phase taught me, my real learning, was about control. Control over one's life, or the illusion of it. Because here's the thing: not everything is in our control. We can't drive everything. Some things happen to us. And some things, we make happen. At that time, when the affiliation was revoked, I could not influence that decision in any way. I wasn't someone who would pick up a placard and march in protest. I didn't have it in me to be part of that noise. I was more of a backseat person, not because I was passive, but because I believed in doing what was in my hands, not disturbing what was not.

So I focused on what I could control. And that was my preparation for the MBA. Nobody else could do that for me. I think a big sense of empowerment, of internal control, came from that. I had time. I could either spend it speculating about what would happen or use it. Others used that time protesting, organizing, and arguing. I decided to study. I knew that if I was going to spend this phase in uncertainty, at least I'd make it meaningful for myself.

That was the core learning for me from that situation: control is limited, but effort isn't. Some things you just have to let be. People have their own karmic journeys. You cannot bear the weight of everyone's battles, and you can't outsource your own either. So I turned inward and doubled down on what I could do.

Adaptability was another big lesson. Situations won't always align with your plans. You won't always get a clean, smooth path. Sometimes, the road cracks under your feet. In those moments, you can't keep crying over the broken concrete. You learn to balance. You learn to shift your weight. You move forward anyway. You adapt. That period, when the college collapsed around us but life continued, taught me that. That's where I understood what it truly means to pivot without panic.

So yes, first came acceptance, and then came forward movement. Control, adaptability, and forward movement became the triad of how I responded to the entire situation. There's a kind of maturity that sets in when you recognize what you can do amidst chaos.

And for me, that "can" was my MBA preparation. I wasn't trying to escape the situation. I was trying to grow despite it.

Now, when I reflect back on that time, I realize how significant it was. It was a test of mindset. I wasn't consciously trying to be strong or composed. I was just acting from instinct. The instinct to keep moving. The instinct to find the next thing worth doing.

And this brings me to something else that was quietly transformative during those days, moving out of the hostel after the first year. Till then, I had been living in the college hostel. Twin-sharing rooms, scheduled mess timings, and a relatively controlled environment. But post-first year, a few of us decided to move out. There wasn't a dramatic reason. I don't even remember why we chose to leave. Maybe it was about independence. Maybe it was about getting better food. Or maybe it was just about creating a space where we could be more ourselves.

We ended up in a paying guest accommodation in Kalkaji, Block A, near Nehru Place. There were six or seven of us, staying in one big hall, sleeping in a row, managing our routines, our meals, our budgets, and our little fights. Suddenly, life became more real. From living with one roommate, I was now living with five or six people, each with a different background, temperament, and habits. And I had to adjust. Learn. Negotiate. Share.

There was one guy, Narendra, who was a year junior to me. He was technically brilliant, especially in networking. A quiet, curious kid, always fiddling with wires, settings, and systems. We had three computers in that one room, and somehow, he managed to set up a mini-network between them. That was the first time I saw the practical side of computer science outside textbooks. How to set up a LAN, share files, and configure IP addresses, I learnt more from observing him in those months than I did from my first semester's computer lab. He had that hunger to explore. And that rubbed off on me. Staying with him and the others wasn't always easy. There were disagreements, frictions, noise, late-night chai sessions, missed alarms, and arguments over cleaning duties. But all of that taught me how to live with people. How to adapt socially, just as I had learned to adapt academically.

It also gave me a strange kind of strength. That I could manage. That I could adjust, survive, thrive, even in a room full of chaos. And I carried that strength back into my MBA prep. Because even CAT prep wasn't a solitary activity. I had to coordinate, share resources, ask questions, and answer others'. But this time, I was more open to people. Not because I had changed fundamentally, but because I had seen the value of shared learning.

So yes, shifting from the hostel to the PG was one of those hidden milestones in my journey. It changed me. It taught me life outside the syllabus. And maybe, in a strange way, it made me more ready for what lay ahead.

All of this, combined, helped me stay steady. Helped me top my college eventually. Even with all the noise, the canceled affiliation, the lost semesters, and the disillusionment, I still managed to stand out. Not because I was the smartest. But maybe because I kept going. I kept recalibrating. Kept moving. Sometimes alone. Sometimes with a few good people.

And I think that's what real learning is. Not just subjects and concepts, but resilience, independence, focus, and emotional maturity. Learning when to act, when to let go, when to adapt, and when to simply stay silent and let life unfold. These weren't in any textbook. But they became the most important parts of my education.

Since I was good at studies, some of my classmates naturally gravitated towards me. When someone is good academically and is also open to making friends, it creates a kind of magnetism. People approach you, not just to talk or pass the time, but with a certain kind of respect. They want help. They want clarity. They want guidance. And slowly, many of these requests turn into bonds. That's how I became close to several classmates. During exams, especially, I was the go-to person. A couple of them had this standard dialogue before every sessional or semester exam: "Vivek, you have to finish your syllabus two days before the exam. We don't know anything, and we need you to teach us in those last two days."

And somehow, this became a pattern. Friendly, yes, but it wasn't just friendship. It was a responsibility. An unspoken commitment that I accepted willingly. It forced me to stay ahead, to finish my own preparation before time. I couldn't afford to lag because others were relying on me. I had to be prepared so that I could help them prepare. And this pressure, strangely, didn't feel like a burden. It felt like a push. A nudge that helped me go deeper into topics I might have otherwise glossed over. It sharpened my understanding.

During those last two days before every exam, our flat or PG room would turn into a mini classroom. I wasn't a teacher, but I ended up taking crash revision sessions. I would tell them which topics were important, what to focus on, what could be skipped, and how to quickly revise chapters. I don't remember the exact hours or schedules, but I do remember the intensity. It was like prepping for war, the exam war, with a group of comrades who trusted me blindly.

Even on the day of the exam, I was expected to be in college at least two hours early. That became a ritual. I would reach early, sit in one of the corners, and soon I would be surrounded by three or four friends, sometimes more, all looking anxious, all seeking last-minute wisdom. They'd bombard me with questions: "Is this coming? Should we skip that? How do you solve this?"

These sessions weren't formal. They were more like focused conversations, where I distilled the syllabus into chunks of relevance and made things easier to grasp. And over time, it gave me a unique edge. Because when you teach others, you don't just revise, you reinforce. You remember better. You see patterns. You learn to simplify. You understand where people get stuck, and that helps you avoid those pitfalls yourself. This habit of finishing early, of teaching, and helping others – it wasn't just good for them. It was a blessing for me.

I think it laid the foundation of my love for continuous learning. It made me crave clarity. I didn't want surface-level knowledge. I wanted to know things in a way that I could explain them. That became my standard of understanding. If I couldn't explain a concept clearly to someone else, I hadn't understood it well enough. This mindset stayed with me long after college. It seeped into my professional life, into my habits, into my way of approaching problems.

Even my final year project and the interviews later benefited from this approach. Because of this habit of helping others and teaching, I was always in the habit of breaking complex things down, of preparing early, and of keeping things simple. And all of this was a ripple effect of those countless evenings spent sitting with my friends, drawing diagrams, writing formulas, and saying, "Don't worry, we'll finish it all."

Looking back, I feel those sessions were more than study hours. They were moments of trust. Of learning how much impact one person can have on others. And more than anything, they were moments of self-growth. Because every time I helped someone understand a tough topic, I grew a little bit more myself. And perhaps, that was the biggest gift of all.

Eventually, all this effort, this consistency, this continuous push to learn deeply and share openly, paid off. I kept topping in college. But the real success was not just in marks or ranks. It was in realizing that growth is not a solitary journey. It is a shared experience. And sometimes, when you teach others, you end up teaching yourself the most.

Chapter 5: The MBA Shift & Recession-Era Struggles

Now let's talk about my MBA journey. I was very clear right from the beginning that I would pursue an MBA immediately after my engineering. On some level, I could not imagine myself being able to take up a job, especially a good one, and then quit it to come back to studying. I was not exactly taught this, and I can still recall that the thought was powerful and unshakable. It was a straightforward plan: complete engineering, appear in CAT, and pursue an MBA. No gap, no break. I was never the kind to take breaks, actually. If I'm in a momentum, I want to keep moving. So I started preparing and eventually got through a college that felt right for me at that time.

I landed at FORE School of Management (FSM), Delhi. It wasn't an IIM, but it had a great reputation and a very solid finance faculty. For me, that was enough. I didn't get bogged down by what others thought was "tier 1" or "tier 2." I always believed, and still do, that your output matters more than the brand on your degree. So I stepped in with that mindset.

When the time came to choose specializations, I was perhaps the only person in the entire batch who picked only one specialization, and that too, full finance. All thirteen subjects were finance. No major-minor business. While others were choosing combinations, Finance + Marketing, Operations + IT, I stood firm. Finance and only finance. No confusion. No dilution.

The MBA curriculum at FSM was structured in a way that the first year was common for everyone. It was a general management foundation year, with subjects from all specializations. We studied the basics of marketing, HR, economics, statistics, accounting, operations, and a bit of IT. That first year gave us a taste of everything. But when the second year began, it was time to commit, and most students picked one major and one minor specialization.

I didn't do that. I took all thirteen subjects from finance. And I still remember the surprise on my professor's face when I submitted my selection. "You sure you want only finance?" he had asked. I said yes. "You'll have no fallback?" he had said. I said, I don't need one.

My logic was simple. First of all, I had a business background, and finance had always fascinated me. I wasn't alien to financial concepts, ratios, balance sheets, cost analysis, investments, and risk; it was like a language I was slowly falling in love with. More importantly, I enjoyed it. There's a huge difference between understanding a subject and enjoying it. Finance made sense to me. It gave structure to the business. It made decisions calculable. It offered predictability in an unpredictable world. I loved the clarity it brought.

Now you might ask, if you were good at computers too, why not IT as a minor? The answer again goes back to a realization I had in engineering. I had become reasonably competent in tech, especially after my Red Hat and networking experience, but I didn't see myself making a career in IT services or tech support roles. And an MBA in IT, frankly, didn't excite me. IT felt like a skill. Finance felt like a discipline. I wanted depth.

Operations were never something I was exposed to properly. Some of the concepts in the first year, like supply chain management, lean processes, and six sigma, sounded interesting, yes, but I didn't feel a pull strong enough. And again, I wanted to go deep, not wide.

Marketing? That was a clear no. First, because I'm an introvert. I'm not someone who thrives on personal attention or enjoys socializing for the sake of networking. I used to see marketing students always in group discussions, role plays, and talking about brands and consumer behavior. It was creative, yes, but I felt it lacked rigor. That depth I talked about? Marketing didn't seem to have it for me. I felt like marketing relied more on intuition and observation than frameworks and analysis. Now, I know better. I've worked with great marketers since, and I've learned that marketing is as analytical as it gets, but back then, that was my perception.

HR? That was a non-starter. Everyone said HR was the fallback if nothing else worked out. I didn't even consider it. It's not that I didn't value human resources as a field; I just didn't see myself ever being in that function. Even today, I believe that if you can't see yourself doing a job for 5-10 years, don't study it.

So that left me with finance, and I dived into it completely. The subjects were fantastic: Corporate Finance, Financial Markets, Investment Analysis, Risk Management, Financial Derivatives, Mergers and Acquisitions, Financial Modeling, the list went on.

Every subject felt like a brick being added to a building I was constructing slowly in my mind. I still remember the first time I created a full financial model from scratch in Excel; it felt like a superpower.

What made finance even more exciting were the professors. One of them, I do not remember the name though, was not just a teacher, but an experience in himself. He could turn the most complex theory into a story. He had worked in investment banking and corporate finance for years before moving into academics, so he brought real-world insights. He once told us, "In finance, it's not about numbers. It's about why the numbers are the way they are." That one line stayed with me. And I think that's where my love for root-cause analysis also took shape.

The other thing that worked in my favor during my MBA was that I was not distracted. I did not belong to politics, cultural committees, placement drama, or even be a loner. I attended, took the classes and did my assignments, and established good relationships with some of the good professors. I made two or three close friends, and I did not have an interest in belonging to any group or gang. I did not dislike people; I was very choosy about the ones that I hung out with. I have been like that ever since school, actually. I am not the loudest voice in the room, but when I talk, I talk with facts.

This clarity, this self-awareness, helped me stay consistent in my MBA. I was not competing with others; I was competing with myself. The goal was simple: learn deeply, get good grades, and get placed in a finance role. I wasn't gunning for the highest-paying job. I was looking for a role that would respect my skills, give me room to grow, and put me in the financial decision-making chain of an organization.

One more reason why I think I did well in the MBA was that I had already built discipline from engineering. Engineering taught me how to be self-sufficient. How to read without a tutor. How to solve problems that nobody else was helping you with. MBA was lighter in comparison, but the trick was in managing time. The projects, the case studies, and the constant flow of assignments could overwhelm someone quickly. But I had my rhythm. I got up early in the morning, studied when my mind was freshest, tried to attend every presentation, and did not miss a single deadline.

And one more thing I would like to mention about that period is an emotional one. I hardly saw my parents once every month. I did not want to miss the point. As usual, my family was supportive. They realised that when I was in, I was in. They trusted me, and that was a lot.

In summary, choosing finance wasn't an accident. I decided to do it consciously based on my personality, interests, and philosophy of doing things profoundly. And so that choice had an impact not only on my MBA itself, but on the basis of my career in future years as well.

So I think, if I had not faced rejection in the early part of my life, that could very well be something sitting silently in the back of my mind, influencing decisions without me consciously realizing it. Rejection is one of those things we're all afraid of until it happens. And in my case, because I hadn't truly faced a full-blown rejection in any academic or professional setting up to that point, I think I subconsciously avoided situations where rejection might be a high possibility. That, I feel now, might have been one of the core reasons that drew me away from sales. Sales, by definition, is about putting yourself out there, hearing "no" repeatedly, and still showing up the next day with the same energy and conviction. At that stage in life, I didn't think I was ready for that.

And just to put that into perspective, from today's lens, ironically, today I *do* sales. Almost every single day. In fact, most of what I do now, professionally, requires reaching out to clients, building trust, talking about my offerings, customizing services, following up, negotiating, essentially all the stuff I once steered clear of. But life has a way of teaching you what you once avoided. The mindset has shifted now. But back then, during my MBA, it was very clear: no sales, no marketing roles for me. I didn't even sit for ICICI Bank's interview process when they came for placements, despite it being one of the earliest and biggest companies to arrive on campus. Why? Because the profile was sales-focused. It was a decision that many questioned, but I was resolute. And that's how the story began to unfold, my story.

Now, here's where it gets interesting. During the first few weeks of my MBA, I met Professor S.K. Gupta. The man, whom I initially assumed was just one of our IT faculty, turned out to be a pivotal figure in shaping my journey ahead. He was everything I wasn't used to: deeply idealistic, principled, disciplined to the last detail, and with a strong expectation of mutual respect. He was not just an academician, but also the placement coordinator of our MBA program.

But at that point, I had no clue he would be so influential in my story. He taught IT in the first year, a subject I was not very emotionally invested in, given my past with computers. Yet there was something in his method, his strictness, his sharpness that stood out. One day, during a regular lecture, he casually asked who among us would like to be the class coordinator for his subject. I don't know why, but I raised my hand and volunteered. Maybe it was instinct, maybe it was my desire to be closer to people who were serious about academics, or maybe I just liked the idea of being involved. Along with another colleague, I was selected as his class coordinator.

Now, this wasn't some fancy title or resume booster. It simply meant that I became his point of contact for anything related to the class, coordinating schedules, assignments, communication with students, and ensuring class discipline. But what it did was much more than logistical support; it gave me **access**. It gave me visibility. It gave me a relationship with someone who held deep respect within the institution.

Our interactions began to increase. Whenever he had a message or an update for the class, he'd call me. If there was a change in the room or a reschedule, I was informed first. This regular connection started building a subtle bond, one that I wouldn't realize the importance of until a storm came knocking.

Around late July or early August, something happened that jolted me hard. The institute issued a circular asking all students to submit their graduation certificates. It was a basic administrative requirement; you couldn't pursue a post-graduate program without completing an undergraduate degree, and they needed to verify the credentials. Fair enough.

But I had nothing to submit.

Because, of course, my engineering college's affiliation had been cancelled. I had no degree. No provisional certificate. Not even a marksheet. And this was not news to me; it had been looming for a while, but that was the moment the fear actually hit me. What was I going to do? I was midway through my MBA semester, sitting in classes, doing well, participating actively, and suddenly, I might be asked to leave? Just like that?

That evening, I remember sitting in the common area, my thoughts racing in all directions. Everyone else had submitted their degrees, moved on. And here I was, about to be disqualified for something that wasn't even in my control.

That night, I didn't sleep much. The next day, I went to Professor Gupta. Not for class coordination. Not for academics. Just to speak. I waited till the class was over, and I nervously approached him.

"Sir, I need to speak to you about something important," I said.

He looked at me calmly and said, "Yes, Vivek?"

I told him everything. About my engineering college. About the affiliation being revoked. About how I still didn't have a degree, and about how the notice had asked us to submit our graduation certificates. I wasn't crying, but my voice was shaking. I still remember how I tried to explain everything in as short a time as possible, trying to sound mature and composed, but the anxiety was visible.

He didn't interrupt. He just listened. And then said, "Why didn't you tell me this earlier?"

"I thought it would resolve... I wasn't sure if it would become a problem."

And then, like only someone with real authority and a calm sense of judgment could, he said, "Don't worry. Go speak to the program director. Tell him your situation. If needed, I'll speak to him too. We'll figure it out."

That moment was like someone had lifted a 50 kg burden off my shoulders. Not because the problem was solved, but because someone who mattered had said, *we'll figure it out.*

With his support, I met the program director and explained everything. He was strict, but understanding. He asked me to formally write an application, explaining the timeline and promising to submit the documents as soon as they were available. He gave me an extension, two months.

That was my first official break, my first institutional support. And it meant the world to me. It was a quiet moment of relief, but it created ripples. Because after that, I doubled down on everything. I attended more diligently. I worked harder on assignments. I made sure that every professor, every coordinator, saw my sincerity. It was my way of saying, "Thank you for trusting me. I won't let you down."

Eventually, the degree situation did resolve. I submitted my provisional certificate within the extended timeline, and things went back to normal. But I never forgot what happened during those two months. The quiet fear. The unexpected support. The learning is that when you're in trouble, don't hide. Reach out to people. Be honest. Tell your story.

And that connection with Professor Gupta? It only grew from there. Not in a transactional sense. He remained someone I deeply respected, someone I often sought guidance from, and someone who reminded me that in institutions, just like in life, it's not just rules that matter. It's people.

MBA wasn't just about finance classes and placements for me. It was about growing up. Understanding systems. Navigating challenges with grace. And most importantly, learning to ask for help and being okay with it.

And yes, that early fear of rejection that kept me away from sales? It still lingered. But cracks had started to form. My comfort zone was slowly beginning to stretch. And as you'll see in the chapters ahead, life had more lessons lined up. Because the real test was not in the classroom. It was waiting just outside.

And I think it was October end now, maybe nearing November, and once again, the reminder came, submission of graduation degrees. This time it wasn't just a routine request. This time, it felt heavier. I had already used my extension once. I had already told my story. And while the institution had been kind, institutions do run on timelines. The nervousness returned. But instinctively, I knew what I had to do. I went back to S.K. Gupta, sir.

He didn't react much. That's how he was, calm, measured. "Go," he said, "Tell them you still haven't received it. Request more time. That's all you can do right now." I nodded. That gave me the strength to face what came next. But this time, it wasn't just the program director I had to meet. The matter had escalated. It was now with someone much more senior, perhaps the dean, or at least someone with greater authority.

She was a lady, and as per common perception, she was strict. I had seen her walk the corridors with an air of discipline. Everyone referred to her with a slight nervousness. And now, I had to go to her office, knock on her door, and explain why I was, again, unable to submit my graduation degree. As I walked into her room, my heartbeat was louder than my footsteps. I greeted her respectfully and began explaining. Slowly, carefully. She listened quietly. No expression. Then she paused. She thought for a moment.

And then came her reply, a condition, not rejection. She said she could give me six more months. But, and this was a big but, the degree, when it finally arrives, must carry the year 2007. My MBA started in 2007. My engineering batch was from 2003 to 2007. The alignment was critical. If my B.Tech degree was dated 2008; the MBA would stand invalid. All of it, this journey, these classes, the assignments, my future, would be nullified by one wrong date. That sentence hit me like a thunderbolt. But at the same time, it gave me hope. She was not closing the door. She was keeping it slightly open, on condition.

I thanked her sincerely. More than relief, I felt responsibility. I have had six months now, but I had to ensure that the degree came with the right year. I had to make this work. And then came another twist, another sign of hope. Around mid-November, our engineering university announced the examination dates for the pending B.Tech semesters. Finally. I remember this announcement like a festival. We were thrilled. Not because we loved exams, but because this was the only way our degrees could be completed. Without these exams, everything we had studied for the past four years would be a memory, not a qualification.

The exams were scheduled from late December onwards. I recall very clearly, they planned five exams across five Sundays. Each exam, one Sunday. One by one. This schedule was not usual, but it worked. And that exam schedule, though simple on paper, played one of the most important roles in my life. Because this was the bridge. This was the moment that stood between the uncertainty of an unrecognized engineering degree and the continuation of my MBA journey.

I look back now and realize how divine that timing was. I had six months. The exams began just in time. The possibility of having the degree dated 2007 was real again. It felt like everything was aligning, finally. God, as always, had been kind. I've said this before, and I'll say it again: life has thrown many challenges at me, but time and again, I've been pulled out of the whirlpool by some invisible hand, some stroke of grace.

The exams were not easy. Not because of the content, I had already studied a lot, and I was confident. But because of the parallel life I was living. On one hand, I was attending MBA classes, preparing for internal assessments, participating in group projects, and coordinating with professors. On the other hand, I was traveling for my engineering exams, revising old concepts, revisiting old notebooks, and appearing for one crucial exam every Sunday. Time was scarce. Energy was stretched. But my mind was focused.

What made it manageable was how I had learned to divide and conquer. During the weekdays, I was a full-time MBA student, participating, preparing, and learning. But once the weekend approached, I would switch tracks, transforming into the engineering student I once was. I would revise the subjects mostly late at night. I would make handwritten notes, remind myself of old formulas, code structures, and theoretical concepts. And then every Sunday morning, I would go appear for the exam. That rhythm went on for five straight weeks.

It was not just an academic test. It was a test of time management, of adaptability, of mental stamina. Each passing Sunday felt like a win. Each finished paper felt like a milestone. Every tick mark brought me closer to the degree. And with every paper, the hope of a 2007-dated degree became stronger. I wasn't alone in this. I had friends who were in the same boat. We supported each other. We discussed subjects. We travelled together. We laughed at the absurdity of the situation, that we were living two lives, writing engineering exams while attending an MBA. But deep inside, we all knew this was our only shot. And we were determined not to miss it.

Amid all this chaos, my MBA performance didn't dip. In fact, I think it improved. It was almost as if this challenge had ignited a new fire in me. I became more alert, more precise, more focused. There was no time to waste. So everything I did, I did with a purpose. And that purpose was survival and success.

Looking back, I think this was another major moment in my life where I experienced what resilience actually looks like. Not in the form of grand speeches or heroic actions. But in the small, invisible choices you make every day, to get up, to show up, to keep going. And that's what I did. I kept going. Some days were exhausting. But never once did I think of quitting. Never once did I consider taking a break from the MBA or skipping an engineering exam. The thought just never occurred to me. The only thought that occurred was: "How do I make this work?"

Because it had to work.

And this phase, the dual life of MBA and B.Tech exams, gave me an invaluable lesson. That no matter how many pieces your life splits into, you can always gather them, realign them, and make a new picture. It may not look perfect, but it will still be yours. And that matters.

And amidst this struggle, something beautiful happened. I started appreciating both my journeys more. I stopped cursing my engineering affiliation issue. I stopped feeling like a victim. Because now, I saw it as a challenge I had accepted. A mission I was close to completing. And I saw my MBA not just as an academic upgrade, but as a second chance that life had given me, a rope to climb out of the hole.

February arrived. The last of the engineering exams concluded. There was a long exhale. It was done. And now, the wait began. The wait for the results. The wait for the degree. The wait for that one piece of paper that had dictated so many of my decisions over the last year. But at least now, I had done everything in my control. The rest was up to the system and fate.

And while that wait continued, my MBA life went on. Classes, assignments, midterms. But now, I carried with me a new kind of confidence. I had faced a unique battle and survived. And I knew, whatever comes next, I'll handle it.

This period, more than any other, taught me what it means to keep walking even when the path is unclear. To believe that if you keep doing your bit, the world will meet you halfway. And in my case, it did.

God helps those who help themselves. My mother always used to say this, repeat it during every hardship, in her calm but firm voice. And this belief, simple as it sounded, was proven time and again. The struggle of parallel engineering exams and MBA classes, the weight of a missing degree, the emotional burden of uncertainty, all of it somehow melted when I saw that final degree. December 2007 was printed on it. And that was it. That was the big solace. The one piece of paper that meant everything, that aligned my past with my present, my B.Tech with my MBA. The universe had once again whispered, "I've got you."

So, yeah. That part was sorted. But just when I thought life was ready to give me a little peace, 2008 walked in. And with it came the recession. We all know what happened. The global economy began crumbling. One big bank, Lehman Brothers, fell. Then it was like dominoes, companies collapsing, jobs vanishing, markets trembling. The fear spread like wildfire, and suddenly, the word 'recession' wasn't just something in the news. It had walked into our classrooms.

And being an MBA student, I knew this. We all knew it. The professors would talk about it in the economics class. The newspapers were filled with grim headlines. Some of our seniors had already started whispering, There are no jobs, placements are frozen, packages are slashed. But even then, I don't remember thinking of it as a personal threat. Maybe it was youth, or maybe it was my tunnel vision on hard work. But I just didn't see it as something that would affect me. I had faith in effort. That's all I knew how to do.

And then came the first company for campus placement, ICICI Bank. They had come with a role for a Relationship Manager. In clear words, it was a sales job. Field sales. Chase targets. Get clients. Cold calls. Rejections. That was the job description. I read it. I absorbed it. And I said, No. I didn't even apply. The forms were to be submitted by noon, and I simply didn't submit them.

That day, just around the time of the application deadline, I was in the department office with Professor S.K. Gupta, again, for some coordination work. Fate loves patterns. He looked at me and casually asked, "Vivek, did you apply for ICICI?" And I said, "No, sir. It's a sales job." What followed was not casual at all.

He snapped. And in that moment, the professor in him disappeared. The mentor stood there, fierce, fiery, protective.

"Beggars are not choosers," he said sharply. "You're sitting in a recession, with zero work experience, and you think you have the luxury to choose?" He wasn't angry out of frustration. He was angry out of care. He wanted me to succeed. And he saw my rejection of that job as arrogance.

He didn't mince his words. "Just get in. Enter the market. Once you're inside, you can do whatever you want. But for now, don't be foolish." I stood there stunned. I had never seen him this stern before. But I understood. In fact, I absorbed every word because in my heart, I respected him deeply. He wasn't just shouting for the sake of it. He was teaching me something that no classroom could. The reality of survival.

So, I walked out, a little shaken, but clearer. I immediately rushed and submitted the form. I don't even remember if it was the same day or the next, but soon enough, the process began. The placement rounds. First, the aptitude test. Then the group discussion. Then the personal interviews.

I had never been great at group discussions. I didn't enjoy cutting people off mid-sentence. I wasn't aggressive. But I did what I could. I spoke. I made my points. I stayed calm. And somehow, it worked. I cleared the GD round. Then came the interview. I don't even remember what they asked. All I remember is that I was honest. I didn't try to pretend to be something I wasn't. Maybe they saw the effort, the consistency, or maybe they saw the desperation well-disguised as discipline.

The results were declared. The placement cell pinned a sheet on the notice board. And there it was. My name. On top. First on the list.

For a moment, I froze. I stared at it again to confirm. And when it sank in, I felt a rush I cannot describe. A cocktail of relief, joy, disbelief, and pride. I had done it. Despite everything, no engineering classes for over a year, no clarity on my degree, parallel exams, recession hanging over our heads, I had done it. I was placed. First from my batch.

That moment meant more to me than anything else. It wasn't just a job. It was validation. It was security. It was hope. And it wasn't just my moment. It was Gupta Sir's too. He had scolded me, yes. But more importantly, he had believed in me. He had nudged me to take that one step. And now, he was elated.

He told the class. He told the faculty. He mentioned it again and again in the next few weeks. And every time he said it, he looked at me with pride. I was his favorite student, not because I topped every test, but because I listened, I grew, and I respected the process. He had no official role in the selection process, no say in the final result. But emotionally, he had a huge role. His presence, his guidance, and his timing it was instrumental.

And that's when I understood something deeper about mentorship. A mentor is not someone who gives you the answers. A mentor is someone who shows you the mirror when you're looking the wrong way. Who doesn't comfort you with lies but pushes you with truths? And in that respect, Gupta sir was the mentor I never knew I needed but always had.

The rest of the MBA placement season was unpredictable. Many companies canceled their visits. Some reduced their offers. Some didn't come at all. But I was safe. I had something. And with that something, I had everything I needed: dignity, confidence, and a platform.

I continued my MBA with even more focus now. I wasn't obsessed with ICICI or the job itself. In fact, deep down, I still wasn't sure if I would enjoy a sales job. But that wasn't the point. The point was, I was in.

And all of it, the degree issue, the recession, the last-minute placement, taught me something I hold dear even today: You may not get to decide your circumstances, but you can always decide your response. And sometimes, the right response is simply showing up, again and again, until luck finds you working.

That phase of life, I can now say, was a masterclass in humility and courage. There were no guarantees. There was no comfort. But there was growth. The kind of growth that builds you from the inside. And no recession, no cancelled affiliation, no missed opportunity can ever take that away from you.

Chapter 6: Rise in the Corporate World

And now came the part I was the most scared about - Group Discussions. I was never very good at them. I didn't like interrupting people, didn't enjoy aggressive debates. But I gave my best. The interview went fine; I was honest, calm, and clear. I didn't pretend to know everything. And then the results were announced.

The list was pinned outside the placement cell. Students crowded around it. I slowly walked up and scanned the list. And there it was, my name. Right at the top. First on the list. I couldn't believe it. I had been selected. I was the first person from my batch to be placed in a company. And not just any year, this was 2008, during one of the worst recessions the world had seen.

That moment hit me like a wave. A mix of disbelief, joy, pride, and a deep emotional surge. I had done it. I had made it. In the face of everything, I had a job. I wasn't someone to jump up and down, but I remember standing there, quietly smiling, holding that moment in my heart.

Gupta Sir was elated. He kept telling everyone. He told other professors, told other students, "Vivek is placed." He had played no formal role in the selection process, but from an emotional and mental perspective, he was a huge part of it. He had seen something in me that I hadn't. And he had pushed me when I needed it most.

That's when I began to understand the deeper truth behind all those management quotes we read in books: attitude matters. Positive behaviour matters. Listening. Respect. Humility. Confidence without arrogance. These aren't just words. These are the silent signals that speak during interviews. When the interviewer sees someone calm, composed, and responsive, they trust. It's not about giving perfect answers. It's about being grounded.

You can train someone on financial models. But you can't train someone to have integrity, to show respect, to take feedback with grace. That's why they say, hire for attitude, train for skills. And maybe that's what worked in my favour. I didn't realise it back then, but I was operating from a space of sincerity, not strategy. And that sincerity was my biggest strength.

With the placement done, the rest of the batch was still sitting with other companies. I was relaxed, but not complacent. And now the wait began for the joining letter. It was March. Then April. And nothing came. The company hadn't sent any communication. It was the recession, after all. Everything was uncertain. And after waiting for over a month, I told myself, I can't just sit idle.

So, I called a friend from my B.Tech class and asked if there was any small work I could do. Anything. I didn't want to waste time. And this friend connected me to his company's CEO. They had a part-time opening for a business analyst. It was a small role, short-term, and the salary was ₹15,000 per month. Pocket money, really. But I didn't think twice.

I went for the interview. It wasn't a big setup. But it was work. It was an experience. It was learning. I took the job immediately. I started working there while waiting for ICICI Bank's joining letter. That small job turned out to be a great decision. I was exposed to real-world problems. I learnt how to write reports, analyse data, and present findings. I got to see how businesses worked. And more importantly, I kept my momentum going. I didn't let the waiting phase become a wasting phase.

Looking back now, it all feels so beautifully timed. The rejection of sales. The scolding. The forced humility. The placement. The wait. The interim job. All of it prepared me. Each part fed into the next. And while it wasn't glamorous, it was real. And real life is never about glamour. It's about grit.

And the biggest lesson of that phase was, movement matters. You may not know where life is going, but keep moving. Sitting idle creates fear. Taking action creates clarity. You may fail, sure. But you will learn. You will grow. And you will be ready when the real thing comes.

So, there I was, an MBA student during the worst global recession, with no degree for the first few months, and no job security even after placement. But I had work. I had learning. And I had a mentor who believed in me more than I believed in myself.

That's all I needed.

At that time, my core intent was to be engaged, to learn, to grow steadily. The glamour of big brands wasn't really something I aspired to. What mattered more to me was peace of mind, financial stability, and the opportunity to contribute meaningfully. And so, the decision became even more complicated. Here I was, offered a decent-paying job at a local firm, working under a boss who valued me, appreciated my work, and was even willing to consider a salary hike to retain me. And then on the other side, there was ICICI, one of India's top banks, a brand that could boost any resume, a structured corporate job in Mumbai with formal training, and a large system in place.

I went back and forth in my head. Every day I thought about it. Every night, I weighed the pros and cons. And the more I thought, the clearer it became that money wasn't going to be the only deciding factor. Yes, ICICI was paying a higher package, but I had to consider the cost of living in Mumbai, the mental stress of adjusting to a new city, the constant race to prove myself in a massive corporate ecosystem, versus working here, at a manageable pace, with a good boss who wanted me to stay. I had already spent three months building that rapport, understanding his expectations, and delivering work that mattered. So, I finally decided to speak to him.

I went to my boss and told him openly, "Sir, I have received the joining letter from ICICI, and while I am happy with the experience here, I cannot ignore the opportunity they are offering. I would like to know your thoughts." He didn't flinch. Instead, he said, "Vivek, I want you to stay. Tell me what it will take." That was powerful for me, not just as a negotiation tactic, but as a moment of genuine validation. I felt seen. I felt respected.

So, I told him honestly, "Sir, if you can offer me a salary that at least gives me parity with ICICI in terms of savings, after rent, commute, and all, I will strongly consider staying." He understood. Over the next couple of days, he got back to me with a counteroffer. He said he would raise my salary to ₹35,000 per month, make it a full-time role, and formalize my responsibilities. He also promised flexibility and continued mentorship. That was enough for me.

I turned down the ICICI offer.

It wasn't a dramatic moment. No speeches. No emotional farewell. Just a quiet realization that I was choosing something unconventional. It felt right. And I've always believed, when something feels right in your gut, it usually is. So I started my journey with this small firm, now formally, now full-time. My role gradually expanded. Earlier, I was just doing online research and making reports. But soon, I began handling more structured responsibilities, coordinating projects, managing virtual teams, preparing presentations, working on financials, and even doing basic strategy support for the US team.

The fact that the boss was sitting in the US helped me gain early exposure to remote collaboration. Back in 2009, remote work wasn't a buzzword. But I was living it. Every morning started with a call, 9:00 am sharp. He would assign the work, give context, and clarify any doubts. And then again, by 6:00 pm, another call, status check, feedback, next steps. That rhythm gave me discipline. It also taught me how to work independently. There was no one micromanaging me. If I didn't work, the work wouldn't move. It was as simple as that.

And soon I realized that the freedom to think, the room to experiment, the chance to make mistakes and learn from them, all of this was priceless. I started reading more about the US market, e-commerce, Amazon selling models, supply chains, SEO, and customer analytics. I was slowly becoming a generalist, a hybrid professional who knew a bit of everything: tech, business, operations, and customer engagement.

One of my earliest tasks was to study book-selling strategies on Amazon. I remember spending hours going through bestseller categories, reading product descriptions, analyzing customer reviews, and tracking price changes. It wasn't glamorous, but it taught me how to notice patterns. It sharpened my observational skills. And over time, I started suggesting ways to improve listings, run offers, and restructure keywords. My boss appreciated it. He even started forwarding my insights to the US leadership.

So, I was reporting to the CEO who was based in of US. He took up whatever suggestions he liked. There was no leadership there. Just forward to his key people who were helping him with the ops and tech.

By the end of six months, I had moved from being a "research analyst" to an "analyst" of sorts, without the title, of course. But the work I was doing had grown. And I was learning by doing. No classroom, no theory. Just pure, hands-on work. And that's where I think my love for practicality in learning began. There's only so much you can pick from books. Real growth comes from execution.

I didn't even realize then how much trust was being placed in me. I was barely 26, but I was running projects. These were foundational moments. Moments that planted seeds of confidence.

There's something else that happened during this phase, something subtle yet powerful. My mindset began to shift. From being a student who wanted a job to being a professional who wanted impact. From thinking about "salary" to thinking about "value." From asking "what should I do" to "how can I do this better." These were internal changes, but they changed everything.

Around October 2009, I started leading a project to revamp the website. We had decided to launch our own e-commerce portal, separate from Amazon. I was coordinating between developers, designers, content teams, and the US office. It was intense. But I loved it. Every challenge felt like a puzzle. And I enjoyed solving it. I didn't know how e-commerce worked. But I learnt. I read blogs, watched YouTube videos, and joined forums. I self-taught myself everything from payment gateways to HTML basics. And I started loving it.

I was speechless.

I was 26. Barely a year out of the MBA. And someone was asking me to lead an office. To hire a team. To manage a business. It wasn't a multinational. It wasn't high-paying. But it was a chance to lead. To build. To create.

I said yes.

Because when life offers you growth, you don't ask for a brand name. You say yes and grow into it.

That's how I became a leader. Not with a title. But with responsibility.

You don't always need to know everything about the subject; you just need to know how to think. That was my first realisation. Going into the interview, I was extremely nervous. I had no prior hands-on experience with SEO; I had only just begun understanding how digital marketing worked, and here I was, expected to evaluate someone else's skill in that very domain. For a moment, I thought of declining, but something within me pushed back. I told myself; this is not about how much I know, it's about how well I ask, how curious I am, and how I can gauge if someone else is bluffing or truly knows their stuff.

So, I prepared the previous night. I read up on whatever I could find about SEO, what on-page SEO, off-page SEO are, what backlinks, keywords, indexing, and meta tags are. I tried to get a feel of what the basics are, so that I don't feel completely lost. And during the interview, I stayed focused on the process, not the technicalities. I asked questions about what he had done in his past job. What tools did he use? Why does he make certain decisions? I asked for examples, real-world work examples. I asked him to explain SEO to a layman. I asked about mistakes he had made and how he had corrected them. And I noticed something interesting; he loved talking about his work. And when someone is passionate and experienced, it comes across. It becomes easier to judge authenticity.

By the end of the interview, I felt like I had just been through a masterclass on SEO. And I wasn't ashamed of it. I acknowledged to myself that the best way to learn something new was to talk to someone who had lived it. That was the day I learnt the power of curiosity over knowledge. And we hired him. Not just because he was competent, but also because we saw that he could fit into our small but growing team.

From there began another phase of my journey. SEO, until then, was a mystery. Suddenly, it became part of my daily work. Since we had hired the guy, it was my job to work with him, understand what he needed, and ensure we were executing his strategies effectively. And this time, unlike the interview, I couldn't just get by with basic knowledge. I had to go deeper. So I did. I started reading SEO blogs, watching videos on link-building strategies, and experimenting with website optimisations. I even created a dummy blog just to test what happens when I change title tags or when I write keyword-rich content.

Within three months, I was confident enough to run small SEO experiments myself. And more importantly, I started asking better questions. I became a better collaborator with the SEO guy because now our conversations were more aligned. I understood his challenges, and I could help him solve them better. That entire phase taught me that we don't need to wait for permission or formal training to learn something new. If the opportunity lands in front of you, grab it. Dive in. You'll float.

Meanwhile, the company kept evolving. My boss would frequently ask me to explore new lines of business. Sometimes he'd ask, "Should we sell digital books?" Another day, it would be, "Can we explore creating an app?" And I had to research and create reports, business models, competitor analysis, and potential customer segments. It wasn't structured work, but it was giving me exposure to many different aspects of business. I was learning how to think about opportunity. I was learning how to weigh risks. I was understanding how decisions are made at the top. And all of this at 26 years of age.

There was one more thing happening in the background. My friends, my MBA batchmates, had all joined big companies, moved to metro cities, and were living the corporate lifestyle. There were moments when I doubted my choices. Sitting in a small office in Delhi, working for a boss who was 12,000 km away, doing 10 different kinds of tasks each day, this wasn't glamorous. It didn't look like "success." There were no fancy cabins, no suits, no big clients. But deep down, I knew I was building a foundation. I knew I was learning things that were hard to get in large, structured firms. I knew I was being given responsibilities that were too big for my title. And somewhere, that gave me comfort.

I remember one of my friends calling me and saying, "Yaar Vivek, tu kya kar raha hai, abhi bhi wahi company mein hai?" And I smiled and said, "Haan, abhi bhi wahi hoon." What I didn't tell him was that in the past six months, I had created a basic marketing plan, a hiring plan, led a team of freelancers, improved our SEO rankings, and learned scripting in Excel. Because sometimes, your path is not meant to be understood by others. You just have to keep walking.

And during this 15-month journey, I had owned everything. From the smallest spreadsheet to the largest business report. I had grown. Not in designations, but in competence. I had become reliable. I had become resourceful. And most importantly, I had become confident.

There was no promotion letter. No employee of the month badge. But I knew what I had achieved. I knew how much I had transformed. And the greatest validation came from my boss himself. During one of our calls, he said, "Vivek, I don't think I could've done this without you. Thank you for everything." I didn't say much. Just smiled and said, "Pleasure's mine, sir."

Because in that one sentence, I saw what mattered more than salary, perks, or brands: the impact.

My journey in that first job taught me that not every opportunity is wrapped in prestige or polish; sometimes, it's hidden in dusty offices, casual meetings, unstructured workdays, and blurry job descriptions. But the richness of the learning can far outweigh the shine of a big brand. That small online bookselling company became the school where I learned real-world problem-solving, people management, and self-driven learning. Yet, by mid-2010, I started to feel the stillness of stagnation creep in. I had squeezed out everything I could from the role. There was no structured growth, no new learning curve, and every day started to look like the previous one.

This feeling of saturation came slowly but clearly. I had taken pride in creating VB scripts to automate Excel sheets, in hiring an SEO professional without having any background in SEO, in learning about SEO hands-on, and helping the company rank better on search engines, but now, the work had plateaued. My tasks were fewer, and while the trust from my boss remained high, the lack of challenge began to gnaw at me. I wasn't growing anymore, and that was unacceptable.

So in May 2010, I made a personal declaration: I would move out in 100 days. I wrote it down. The countdown began. It wasn't anger. It wasn't frustration. It was clarity. When you're no longer growing, you're shrinking. And I didn't want to shrink. Not when I was just getting started in my career. I started updating my resume, actively looking for job openings, and applying to companies that would stretch me. I knew the next role wouldn't be easy, especially not if I wanted to leave the comfort of a job where my boss trusted me, where I worked from near home, and where I was already drawing a decent salary.

But staying was not an option.

In August 2010, I received an offer from a company based in Faridabad. It was a tougher setup. It meant leaving the comfort of my home and moving to a PG accommodation. The daily commute would no longer be four kilometers, but an entirely different city altogether. The new job didn't come with all the answers, but it came with one thing I was craving: learning. It offered structured work, new responsibilities, a different environment, and most importantly, an unfamiliar domain where I could grow again.

It wasn't just a job switch. It was a mindset switch.

I informed my current boss about my decision. He was not happy. He had grown used to me being his go-to person. He didn't need to explain twice. He could depend on me. I could sense that he was disappointed, not because of losing an employee, but because he would have to once again go through the cycle of trusting someone new, training them, and hoping they stayed.

But he understood. He asked me, "Is it something I did wrong?" And I told him with complete honesty, "No, sir, not at all. It's just that I am not learning anymore." He respected that. He didn't try to stop me beyond one gentle nudge. That final moment of mutual understanding made me realise something important: good leaders don't hold people back. They let them grow.

Leaving that job was a hard decision, but it was mine. And that became another recurring theme in my life: choosing. Life always gives us situations where we can either stay still or move forward. But what most people fail to realise is that staying still is also a choice. And if you're not making the choice consciously, someone else is making it for you.

So far, in my short career, I have made three bold choices. First, joining a local company for Rs. 15,000 rather than waiting idly for ICICI's joining letter. Second, choosing to continue with that local company by negotiating a salary of Rs. 35,000, instead of chasing the big brand that everyone around me thought I should join. And third, deciding to leave that company when I realised I had stopped learning, even though it meant moving out of my comfort zone.

None of these choices came with a guarantee. I didn't know what the right decision was at any point in time. But I made them based on what I valued most: learning and growth.

Over the years, I've heard many people say, "I don't know what to do. I'm stuck." And my only advice to them has been: make a choice. Choose something. Because even if it turns out to be the wrong choice, at least you'll learn from it. At least you'll move. Life is not a spectator sport.

The first job taught me another crucial lesson: the power of resilience. Whether it was taking an interview with a person more experienced than me, navigating the expectations of a US-based boss with minimal supervision, or learning SEO and Excel on the fly, I was constantly thrown into deep waters. And I swam. Not because I had a choice, but because I chose to stay afloat. Every discomfort was a lesson. Every challenge was a class. And I passed, without any textbook, without any formal training.

Another important learning was the value of resourcefulness. I didn't have everything figured out. But I was always figuring things out. Whether it was learning Excel automation by observing other people, or understanding how SEO works by working alongside the hired professional, or preparing for interviews of skills I didn't possess, I was always building myself, bit by bit, byte by byte.

If I look back now, that first job became the real launchpad of my professional career. Not because of what I earned, not because of what I achieved, but because of what I became. I became someone who could adapt. Someone who could learn. Someone who could take initiative even when there were no instructions. And more importantly, someone who could trust his own decisions.

Even when there was no obvious path ahead, I created one. Even when I had no experience, I stepped up. And even when comfort tempted me, I chose growth.

That's the legacy of my first job. It wasn't written in gold. It wasn't viral on LinkedIn. It didn't give me awards or titles. But it gave me confidence, the kind that comes not from achievements, but from lived experiences.

And with that confidence, I took my next step.

Ready to walk away from comfort, into something more uncertain, more demanding, but also more exciting. Faridabad awaited. And I was no longer the same person who had hesitated during my first group discussion. I was someone who had seen his own transformation. And once you've seen yourself grow, there's no going back.

Chapter 7: From Overwhelmed Manager to Strategic Leader: A Coaching Transformation Story

There was no objective towards either title or salary; the objective was just to move on, to learn, and to do everything I took on with the greatest sincerity. I wanted to complete a task that was on my desk, whether at official or unofficial time, like it was mine, like I belonged to it. I began using that mentality as my fuel. I used to spend so many evenings converting to late nights in the office, not because I was made to stay there, but because I did not feel like leaving something undone.

Work-life balance is a question that people will frequently request, and I do not think that there is a single answer that works. To me, at that early and middle career stage, work was life. I was unmarried, I had no kids, and I was hungry, not for rewards, but for ownership. So, if there was time, I invested it back into work, and that consistency showed. Slowly but surely, people began to trust me with more responsibility, not because I was loud or assertive, but because I was there, dependable, and predictable in my performance.

And of course, along with this drive came an emotional connection to work that isn't talked about much. I didn't do tasks mechanically. Every little thing that I was doing, I always thought about its business impact. Such questions as, why do I do this? Or how will this assist the company or our customers? We're being asked. The difference is what you feel emotionally, that is, really caring. It's what elevates a worker into a contributor, and later, into a leader.

Another key element that helped me in those days was documentation. I was a big believer in writing things down. I didn't trust memory alone. If I learned something new, I'd note it. If a colleague explained a process, I'd draft a document around it. Soon, I became the go-to person for SOPs, process flows, and presentations. People knew that if Vivek was doing something, there would be a written, documented, structured version of it. This habit helped me transition from operations to strategy in many roles.

This brings me to another point: initiative. No one had to tell me to write those documents. No one assigned me the task of cleaning up process flows. I just saw the gaps and acted on them. Not once did I think, "Why should I do this if it's not in my KRAs?" Instead, my lens was: "If I can do it, and it needs to be done, then let me do it." That ownership attitude, I now realise, is rare, and it sets you apart. It makes you indispensable.

But of course, there were tough times too. There were projects that failed. There were colleagues who didn't match the same energy. There were weeks where everything seemed blurry and motivation dipped. But during all those phases, what kept me grounded was the thought that I am here to learn and contribute. The rest, recognition, promotions, applause, they all come and go. But learning sticks.

This drive toward learning also manifested in my interest in cross-functional work. If I were in marketing, I would want to know what sales were doing. If I were in the product, I wanted to know what tech was building. If I were in operations, I would want to understand customer support metrics. I never kept my scope narrow. The idea was not to interfere but to understand. Because unless you understand the ecosystem you are part of, your own performance will always remain limited. You'll operate in silos, and silos don't scale.

This interest also made me establish casual relationships with others in different departments over time. I would talk to them, not only on work-related issues, but what they liked, what they were having difficulties with, what they were seeing change in the company or in the market. These conversations became my real MBA. I was learning real business insights not from books, but from people who were living it. That's when I also realized the value of listening. Many people talk, but very few truly listen. And when you listen without jumping to respond, people open up. You earn trust. And trust is the first step toward influence.

One more trait that played a huge role was my comfort with ambiguity. In the corporate world, not everything is black or white. You don't always get crystal-clear instructions. There are gaps. There are grey areas. There are moments when no one knows what to do next. I learned early on that those moments are not obstacles; they're opportunities. If you can walk into ambiguity and bring clarity, you become a leader automatically.

People start looking up to you because you provide direction when the compass seems broken.

There was a time, I remember vividly, when a high-stakes project was failing due to inter-departmental miscommunication. Everyone was defending their own turf. Meetings were happening, but outcomes were missing. I stepped in, not because someone asked me to, but because I had context from all departments. I had been listening. I had been documenting. And in one meeting, I drew a simple diagram on the whiteboard explaining the issue and suggesting a flow. People paused. And then they nodded. That small act of bringing clarity to chaos made a deep impression. It wasn't part of my job, but it became part of my growth.

I think all of this boils down to intent. If your intent is to help, to solve, to grow, then people will see it. You don't have to market yourself too much. Your work will become your brand. And brands built on intent are far stronger than ones built on noise.

Now, one may ask, what about personal life? What about family time? Didn't I miss out? Perhaps yes. There were weekends sacrificed. There were social plans cancelled. There were family gatherings where I showed up late or mentally absent. But I think it's also about phases. My phase then was about building myself. Today, I have more balance. But back then, I needed that intensity to shape the foundation.

Looking back, all the small habits, writing things down, being curious, taking initiative, working beyond hours, listening to people, staying present, and embracing ambiguity, they compounded. And that's the beauty of habits. You don't realise their impact day by day, but over months and years, they change your trajectory completely.

No single habit can make or break your career. But a combination of the right habits, repeated consistently, can take you to places even talent alone cannot.

And that's what I want to end this part with: consistency beats intensity. You don't need to burn out in one quarter. But you do need to show up every day. Learn something new every week. Offer help even when it's not asked for. Listen when others are too busy talking. Stay late when a project needs a little more time. And most importantly, don't wait for perfect clarity. Act with whatever clarity you have.

Because movement creates momentum. And momentum, even slow, is still forward.

There's a fundamental truth I've come to believe deeply over the years: anything worth excelling in demands time. Not just effort. Not just skill. But pure, unfiltered time. You can't shortcut mastery. You can't chase greatness in 8 hours. If you want to be good, average effort may suffice. But if you want to be very good, if you want to rise above the noise, then time is your biggest investment. And it's not even about staying late at the office. It's about how much of your own self you are willing to pour into your work. How much of your energy, your focus, your hours, are you truly willing to give?

For me, this was never a rule. It was instinct. I didn't follow the clock; I followed my work. I was an early riser, not because it was trendy or because someone advised me to be one, but because the early hours gave me uninterrupted space to think, plan, and act. Most of my life, I've woken up around 4 AM. And once I was up, I didn't spend time scrolling or strolling, I opened my laptop. I checked my emails. I cleaned up my to-dos. I reviewed yesterday's work. I planned today. That first hour, between 4 and 5 AM, was the most powerful part of my day. My brain was fresh, distractions were zero, and clarity was maximum.

And none of this was counted as 'office hours'. I wasn't doing it for visibility. I wasn't trying to prove a point. I just liked being in control. I liked the feeling that I was not chasing work, but leading it. That nothing was pending, nothing was lost in the inbox, no one was waiting for a reply, no deliverable was hanging in the air. That control gave me peace. And peace, ironically, made me sharper. It gave me bandwidth to take on more, to go deeper into what I was doing.

Most people think time management is about doing more in less time. For me, it was about giving more time to the things that matter. It was never "how quickly can I do this," but "how well can I do this." Speed came later. First came the quality. First came the thought. First came the dedication to do something that I would be proud of when I look back.

And when people asked me, "How do you manage so much?" the answer was simple: I didn't put a limit on myself. I didn't stop at 6 PM just because the office closed. I didn't say, "I'll get to this tomorrow," if I had the mental space to finish it today. It wasn't about being a workaholic. It was about being committed. Committed to the outcome. Committed to my name on the task. That subtle pride of doing something well, that drove me more than appraisals, more than awards.

One of the biggest advantages of this mindset was that I started seeing gaps faster than others. When you're deep into your work, you start noticing patterns. You start noticing what's not working. And that's how I started asking for more work, not because I was free, but because I was aware. Aware of what's broken. Aware of where things could be improved.

I remember in my first company, when the official workload started reducing, I didn't sit idle. I learned Excel. Then I learned automation using VBScript. Then I went into SEO. Then I interviewed someone more experienced than me in SEO, and learned how to interview even when you don't know the subject. I didn't wait for someone to hand me learning on a silver platter. I went looking for it. I created my own learning environment.

And that stayed with me in every company I worked for. Whenever I sensed a dip in my engagement, my energy didn't drop; I simply redirected it. I found something new to learn. Some new angle of the business to understand. Some new tool to master. This habit, of seeking learning rather than waiting for it, was one of the most powerful contributors to my growth.

Another powerful habit was initiative. I never believed in "wait for your turn." If I saw something broken, I tried fixing it. If I saw a colleague stuck, I offered help. If there was an internal presentation and someone needed slides, I pitched in. If a process seemed clunky, I'd sit with the stakeholders and map it out. I didn't wait for permission. And because I was never running short of energy or time, I could do this on top of my responsibilities. That's when you build trust. Not by doing what's told. But by doing what's needed.

You see, no one will ever stop you from going above and beyond. But no one will push you either. That push has to come from within. And I had that push. I still have it.

And another big lesson that shaped me during this time was about what separates good professionals from great ones. I observed that it's not IQ. It's not a college pedigree. It's not even communication skills. The real differentiator is ownership. Great professionals take responsibility like it were their own business. They don't say, "This isn't my department." They say, "This affects our outcome. Let's fix it." And that's how I started treating every project as if my reputation depended on it. Because it did.

Even the little things mattered. Like how I wrote emails. I always took extra care to ensure my emails were crisp, respectful, and clear. Because I believed people judge your thinking by the way you write. So every sentence was deliberate. Every word had a reason. Even in internal notes, I'd keep a structure: what the problem is, what's been done, what help is needed. Clarity builds confidence. And when people start trusting your clarity, they involve you in bigger things. That's how I grew, one email, one deliverable, one conversation at a time.

And none of this happened in isolation. While I worked on my own growth, I was always mindful of the people around me. I truly believed that you grow faster when the people around you grow with you. So if I had a shortcut to something, I shared it. If I figured out a better template, I circulated it. If I cracked a client pitch structure, I taught it to my juniors. That created a reputation of being someone who uplifts, not competes. And in the long run, that brings people to your side when you need support. You can't be a one-person army in corporate life. You need allies. You need a network of trust.

So all this boils down to just one core idea: never outsource your growth. Don't wait for your manager to assign you a challenge. Don't wait for HR to plan a training program. Don't wait for the company to sponsor a certification. If you feel you need it, go get it. Time, energy, learning, visibility, it's all in your hands if you decide to own it. And once you take ownership, everything changes. Because you're no longer reacting to life. You're designing it.

I often get asked, "What's the secret to consistent growth?" And I always say: Don't stop building even when no one's watching. That's the secret. Build when it's quiet. Build when it's boring. Build when it's thankless. Because that's when real growth happens, not in the limelight, but in the shadows. Not in applause, but in solitude.

And so, my philosophy has always been simple: do the work, love the work, own the work. You do this long enough, and success, whatever shape it takes, has no choice but to follow.

In a big company, surrounded by sharp minds and tight processes, the only way to grow fast is to create your own momentum. And I knew this. I knew that if I was to move ahead, I couldn't just wait to be noticed; I had to make them notice me. It wasn't about being loud; it wasn't about showcasing myself at every meeting; it was about value. If I could add more value, if I could take on more responsibility without being asked, I knew I would rise.

It was sometime in 2012. I had completed over 15 months at IndiaMART. I remember joining this place in December 2010. I was working on one product, and I felt I had reached a solid grip. I knew the product inside out. KPIs were stable. Processes were refined. I was handling escalations well. But 20% of my time still remained underutilized. So I thought, why wait for someone to assign me more work? Let me go and ask for it.

But I didn't just go to my reporting manager. I went two levels up. Straight to the Chief Product Officer. Skipped the conventional route. Skipped hierarchy. I went to him and said, "I feel I can take more. If you think I'm not doing justice to the current product, test me. Ask me anything. And if I fail, I'll walk back and never bring it up again."

He smiled. I remember that moment. He smiled in surprise, not just at the confidence but at the audacity. But I was serious. I wasn't trying to show off. I was genuinely ready. And I told him this wasn't about ambition. It was about potential. If there was more I could do, I wanted to try. That's it.

After that conversation, every Monday morning, at 8:30 sharp, I would be outside his cabin. No follow-up emails. No pestering.

Just a silent reminder, I'm still here. Ready for more. Week after week. Ten weeks passed. Twelve, maybe. And one fine day, he looked at me and said, "The way you've been chasing me for more work... I'm giving you three more products."

That was a big moment. From one product, I now had four. It wasn't just a workload increase; it was a vote of trust. A signal that I had arrived. I was ready for more complex challenges. And I didn't take that lightly. I didn't jump in with pride. I walked in with humility. I knew that this meant more eyes, more expectations, and much more scrutiny. I had to earn the right to stay at this level now.

The above did not happen. The CEO himself had played a role in giving me the 4 products. In fact, by that time, he had known my work well.

That day when the CEO came in, I was at my workstation in a corner and was meeting with my team. Larger team it was then.

So he decided to give me a cabin and pointed to a nearby cabin and asked me to use that now.

For many senior folks on the floor, it ruffled feathers. Someone junior, someone newer, now had a cabin. But for me, it was never about pride. I treated it with even more responsibility. I knew that when people are watching you, they aren't just watching your results. They are watching your attitude. One arrogant sentence, one dismissive gesture, and all the good work gets tainted. So I made it a point to be even more respectful. Not performative respect, but genuine humility. Because the moment your tone changes, your growth becomes someone else's irritation.

In fact, I learned very early that success is fragile. When you rise, people expect you to change. And if you let pride slip in, even subtly, you lose people. So I stayed conscious. Deliberately conscious. To never speak in a tone that would make others feel small. To never project myself as "above." And that is not just good ethics. It's a good strategy. Because corporate success is not just about what you deliver, it's about how you make people feel when you're delivering it.

Alongside this, another powerful lesson came from feedback. I was inherently an emotional person. I took my work very seriously. So when someone corrected me, or worse, scolded me, I would take it to heart. I would replay those conversations in my head. Especially when the CEO raised his voice at me, I would feel deeply impacted. But one day, after a meeting, he walked up to me and said, "Vivek, don't marry your scolding. Just take the feedback and improve."

That changed everything.

Because he was right. He wasn't attacking me. He was challenging me. And if I chose to look at every piece of harsh feedback as an emotional event, I'd never grow. But if I took it as a mirror, as a push to sharpen myself, I would keep evolving. So from that day onward, I stopped feeling scolded. I started listening to it. And working on it. That shift in mindset created a massive impact.

By late 2012, things escalated further. The Chief Product Officer, who had mentored me and entrusted me with more work, decided to move on from the company. And just like that, I was reporting directly to the CEO.

That was another inflection point. Reporting to the CEO is not a badge; it's a battleground. You can't hide. You can't be vague. You can't delay. You either perform, or you're replaced. And I knew that. So I braced myself. I didn't get scared. But I got serious. More serious than I had ever been.

Every meeting now was with the topmost leadership. Every conversation was sharper, quicker, and more outcome-driven. There was no hand-holding. No reminders. You had to own your space. And owning meant being proactive, precise, and prepared at all times. I still remember how my evenings changed. Earlier, I would just review tasks. Now, I would rehearse answers in my head. Anticipate questions. Back up my data. Prepare my own slides. Practice my points. It was no longer about doing the job. It was about defending the job. Earning it every single day.

But this also came with learning that no MBA or training program teaches you: executive presence. How do you speak? How do you walk into a room? How do you present yourself in front of a CXO panel? What do you say, and what do you hold back? These things matter more at senior levels than your actual slide decks. I began learning that quickly by observing. By reflecting. By experimenting. And over time, I evolved.

Another big advantage I had was my comfort with data. I never shied away from going deep into numbers. And when you report to the CEO, your ability to convert data into decisions becomes your biggest asset. He doesn't want noise. He wants clarity. And the faster you can give it to him, the more he trusts you.

So yes, 2012 was a year of transition. From a mid-level product manager to a CXO's right hand. From working under supervision to leading with accountability. From being managed to managing up. And every day, I reminded myself, this is a privilege. Don't let it slip.

I didn't take weekends off unless absolutely needed. I didn't say, "I'm done for the day," just because the clock said so. Because I believed then, and still do, that real growth is not a ladder. It's a spiral staircase. It turns, it twists, sometimes it's hard to see what's ahead. But the only way up is to keep moving, keep learning, and most of all, keep contributing more than what is asked of you.

And that's the story of how I grew, not by luck, not by title, but by choosing to do more, before being asked.

Chapter 8: Core Principles & Mindset

My next chapter of life was at ICICI. I was offered a salary of fifty thousand per month. However, I didn't join that company. I instead joined a local company at forty-five thousand. People asked me why. Why would you give up more salary for less? But my answer was simple. I was looking for a place to learn. And then when I left there after fifteen months to join another company, where I stayed for just three months, I joined there at forty-two thousand. And when I decided to leave there and come to IndiaMART, I joined again at forty-two. So initial one and a half years, I had a de-growth from fifty to forty-two. Why? Just because I was not getting a good place where I could learn well.

I think this became an important reason for my strong foundation. A foundation based purely on learning and thriving. One day, soon after I had started reporting directly to the CEO, which was right after October 2012, I was working on a project. My CEO was waiting for a particular feature to be launched in that new project. Somehow, I got stuck in too many other things going on within the same project, other features, other tasks. And one day, he called me up and asked, "Vivek, why hasn't this happened yet?"

I said, "No, sir, I was working on some other feature."

And then came the scolding. The kind where the volume and the intensity leave no room for misunderstanding. He asked me why again. I told him the other team had asked me to help them, so this had been pending. His voice rose. "I will get it done myself. I will do the programming myself!" That was the softest way I can put it; in reality, he was loud and firm. I think that was the first time I was scolded so badly.

This is the challenge of working directly with the CEO. CEOs don't have patience for delays. They don't want work done tomorrow; they want it done yesterday. I was sad, emotional. But the next day, when he came to the office, he sat with me for a good forty-five minutes. I remember this vividly. He taught me the importance of prioritization. He explained the Priority Matrix: important versus urgent. The Eisenhower Matrix. He showed me how every task falls into one of four quadrants: important and urgent, important but not urgent, urgent but not important, and neither important nor urgent. He said, "You must always do first what is important and urgent."

The work I was doing had been important, but not urgent, compared to the feature he was waiting for. That lesson stuck.

But my growth at IndiaMART was not only about prioritization. Time management played a huge role. I was always good at time management, but more than that, it was about utilizing time to the best. Finding opportunity. Seeing time not in big chunks of hours, but in slots of five minutes.

If you have to go somewhere at eight o'clock, and you get ready by 7:55, you have five minutes. Use them. Many tasks don't require an hour; they need three or four minutes. These are small fillers. Use them well. As James Clear says in his book *Atomic Habits*, break down big jobs into small, two-minute actions. Once you have broken a task into a two-minute job, you can fit it into those spare minutes. For example, cutting your nails. It takes three minutes. Reading a short news brief. Writing a quick email.

I applied this in my work. And there was one incident that reinforced it for me. I was in a review meeting. My team's project was being reviewed. Four or five senior heads of departments were present, my peers in designation, though more experienced than I. The CTO and the CEO were also there. The CEO started by mentioning a news article from that day. He asked who had read it. Not many engaged. He asked me. I said, "No, sir." And right there, in front of everyone, he pointed it out.

That day I decided I must be more updated. From the next day, I stopped driving to the office and started using cabs. Uber had just become common around 2016–2017. From November 2017 onwards, I used the 30-minute cab ride in the morning to read the newspaper, and the ride back in the evening to check emails or make important calls. That was one extra hour of productivity every single day. Small change, big impact.

Then there was integrity. One of IndiaMART's core values is TRIP: Team-Work, Responsibility, Integrity, and Passion. For me, the order was different: Integrity first, then Passion, then Responsibility, and finally Teamwork. Integrity is more than honesty. It's being truthful in all aspects, to others, to the organization, and most importantly, to yourself.

Once, I told my CEO that I regard integrity as the highest value. He agreed and added something that stayed with me. He reminded me of the Mahabharata, of Yudhishthira's half-truth that was used as a strategy to defeat Dronacharya. Even that, he said, was a calculated move in a war, but in corporate life, if people can trust your word without question, you will always stand out.

Decision-making was another crucial factor in my growth. As you rise in your career, you become a key decision-maker. This means knowing not just how to decide, but also why you're deciding. Many people jump straight to the "what" without understanding the "why." I always made it a point to first understand the purpose, what we wanted to achieve.

If the objective is wrong, the decision will fail, no matter how smart it looks. That's why whenever I communicated a decision, whether in an email or a meeting, I started with the purpose and the expected result.

But decision-making isn't always about data. Sometimes, too much data leads to paralysis. In many situations, speed matters more than depth. There were moments when I relied on intuition, informed gut feeling. I would look at some data, do a few quick calculations, consider the permutations, and then decide. This balance between speed and depth was critical. Go too deep, and you lose time. Go too fast without enough depth, and you risk making errors. The art lies in knowing what is needed in the moment.

And that art, I think, was one of the reasons I was trusted with bigger roles at IndiaMART.

I think looking back, the real thread through all of this was not just about leadership or career shifts, but about energy, the quiet, invisible current that runs through every conversation, every meeting, every late-night call. I didn't always see it in the beginning. Back then, I thought leadership was about decisions, strategy, and execution. But during those months of four-hour CXO meetings, when fatigue sat on our shoulders like a weight and the to-do lists grew longer instead of shorter, I began to notice something deeper. The days when I walked into those calls calm and grounded, my team worked with a certain clarity, as though my stillness had given them permission to slow down and think. And on the days when I was anxious, when my voice was a little too sharp or my breathing too fast, they absorbed that too. It spread like a quiet virus, except instead of coughing and sneezing, people stumbled in their judgment, made avoidable mistakes, and second-guessed themselves. It taught me one of the most important lessons I've ever carried: a leader's inner state is contagious, and you have to guard it like it's your most precious asset.

The pandemic was a relentless teacher. Not just in terms of business urgency, but in the way it stripped us down to the essentials of human connection. Managing seventy-five people remotely, in a world where internet routers were failing, electricity was disappearing without warning, and everyone was worried about the health of their families, that wasn't just management. That was human stewardship. I learned that during a crisis, people don't work for a company; they work for you. They trust the person they're reporting to, not the logo on their payslip. And trust is built not just on capability, but on how you make them feel. The irony was that while the business needed speed, the people needed patience. While targets demanded pressure, the humans behind the laptops required empathy. Walking that tightrope without falling off either side became my main job.

Every morning began with my team meeting, every late morning rolled straight into the CXO war room, and every night bled into the next day's prep. Sleep was a luxury, but purpose made up for it. Even when I caught COVID a year into it, quarantined alone in another flat while my wife and daughter were themselves unwell in our home, I kept the calls going. Not because anyone asked me to, but because there was this unspoken accountability I felt toward my role, my team, my part in keeping the wheels turning. Sometimes I think those days cracked something open in me. I discovered reserves of endurance I didn't know I had, the ability to push past physical fatigue and keep my composure under sustained stress. But perhaps more importantly, I learned where my boundaries truly were, and how to stretch them without breaking.

It wasn't just the big dramatic moments that stayed with me. It was the small, almost mundane obstacles that turned into daily lessons. Upgrading from my sluggish home computer to my office machine, then finally to a 27-inch Mac so I could work more efficiently. Realizing that without a router UPS, even the best Mac was useless during power cuts, and rushed out to buy one. Coordinating ERP access on mobile devices so employees stranded at home could keep processes moving. Hunting for medicines during shortages, arranging quarantines, juggling technical challenges with human emergencies. It was as if life had decided to give me a crash course in adaptability. And strangely enough, I enjoyed it. Not the illness or the fear, but the growth. The way it sharpened my decision-making and forced me to lead in ways I never had before.

By the time the world began to breathe again, something in me had shifted. I'd proven to myself that I could operate under fire. And yet, I also felt this pull, a whisper that maybe it was time to build something of my own. In 2022, I came close to stepping out, drawn toward the startup energy that was exploding post-COVID. Ideas swirled in my head, from tutoring platforms to insurance tech, fueled by stories of entrepreneurs who had turned lockdown problems into billion-dollar solutions. My boss, who had known me for over a decade, was shocked when I told him I was thinking of leaving. My coach, Mr. Dhruv Prakash, listened more quietly, then asked the question that stopped me: "Have you started anything yet?" The truth was, I hadn't. It was more of an urge than a plan, a restlessness that I couldn't yet channel into something tangible. His advice was simple: wait. Stay. Build clarity before you leap.

I listened. But the urge didn't go away. In 2023, the startup itch came back, this time with an insurance app idea that felt more concrete. My boss saw the determination in me and agreed to a transition plan, handing over my CIO role to a successor while giving me the freedom to test my concept. For a couple of months, I tried to balance both worlds. And then reality set in. Two young kids at home, a demanding startup idea, and the remnants of a corporate role, it was a triangle I couldn't hold together without dropping something important. The one thing I refused to drop was my family. I shelved the startup dream, stayed on in a new capacity, and told myself I'd find another outlet for that restless creative energy.

That outlet came almost quietly. Coaching had crossed my radar before; someone had even offered to train me during COVID, but at the time, legal and contractual boundaries made moonlighting impossible. Now, with more flexibility, I started exploring it seriously. I'd been mentoring people for years, guiding younger colleagues, offering perspective when they were stuck. But professional coaching? That was something I'd only seen from the other side, as a coachee. And yet, the impact my own coach had on me was undeniable. If I could give that to someone else, to help them see themselves more clearly, to unlock choices they didn't know they had, that felt like a purpose worth chasing.

So in September 2023, on my birthday, I landed in Mumbai for the first leg of my coach training. Three days of immersion that turned out to be nothing like I'd imagined. I learned very quickly that coaching wasn't mentoring. It wasn't about giving advice or sharing your own stories. It was about asking the kind of questions that peeled back the layers of someone's thinking until they found their own answers. It was about deep listening, not just to the words but to the pauses, the hesitations, the emotions hiding between sentences. It was about helping someone shift, not because you pushed them, but because you held up a mirror they couldn't ignore.

Those three days, and the follow-up sessions two months later, changed my definition of impact. I'd always believed values drive behaviour, but coaching took me deeper; it showed me how identity shapes values, how mindset shapes possibility. I saw it happen in real time during peer sessions, where one person would start guarded and sceptical, and by the end be in tears, having committed to a decision they'd been avoiding for years. And the transformation wasn't because someone had given them "gyan." It was because someone had been fully present with them, without judgment, holding the space for their own clarity to emerge.

For me, the biggest internal shift came when I addressed one of my own sticking points in a peer session: my aversion to sales. In my second job years ago, trying to bid for projects online had cemented my belief that I was not a "sales person." Coaching challenged that. In that session, I reframed it, not as selling, but as serving. If coaching could genuinely help someone, then offering it wasn't pushing a product; it was offering a gift. That single shift in perspective was liberating.

By the time I'd logged close to ninety coaching hours, I knew this wasn't just a side interest. This was something I could do anywhere, at any stage of life, even from a hospital bed if it came to that. All I needed was someone willing to be coached and the space to be present with them. And yet, inside the corporate structure, I couldn't give it the time and breadth it deserved. When I told my boss I wanted to dedicate more of my time to coaching, he was supportive but clear: if I wanted to expand it beyond the company, I'd need to step outside.

It wasn't an easy decision, but it felt inevitable. The work I'd done as CIO had been meaningful, but this was a different kind of meaning, one that lit me up in a way quarterly reports never could. Before leaving, I made sure to complete my certification, clearing the assessments and the final exam so that I could walk out not just with a title, but with the credibility and skill to back it up. I left IndiaMART on good terms, with gratitude for the years of growth and the relationships that had shaped me. And I stepped into the next chapter of my life, a chapter where the bus I was driving wasn't a corporate transformation train, but the quiet, powerful vehicle of human transformation, one conversation at a time.

Decision-making, I realized over the years, is not merely about what choice you make, but when you make it. Timing, in many ways, is the invisible hand that shapes the outcome of any decision. I've often said that a decision taken at the right time is the right decision; take it too early and you might face resistance or lack of readiness, take it too late and you miss the moment entirely. The principle is no different from the old saying, justice delayed is justice denied. In leadership, a delayed decision is often as bad as a wrong decision. Over time, I trained myself to handle timing in two distinct ways. First, if a decision was pending on my desk, it would never gather dust. I would prioritize it, assess the facts at hand, and act promptly. A leader who delays decisions creates bottlenecks and demotivates the team. Second, there's the equally important instinct of knowing when *not* to decide. Sometimes the right move is to wait, wait for data, for alignment, for the right environment where the decision can be accepted and executed effectively. This sense of timing, this balance between immediate action and strategic delay, is what adds maturity to leadership. It allows you to weigh not just the needs of the moment but the overall health and direction of the organization.

Linked closely to timing is the lens through which decisions are made, short-term fixes versus long-term solutions. Many people default to patchwork because the pressure to "solve it now" is immense. The problem is that such fixes often create new issues down the line. My approach, wherever possible, was to favor long-term resolutions. For instance, during root cause analysis (RCA) sessions, while the team focused on putting out the immediate fire, I would push further, what can we do to ensure this problem never returns? Sometimes the answer meant significant changes: rewriting a process, restructuring a team, or even modifying system architecture. These were harder, slower, and more resource-intensive choices, but they built resilience. I firmly believe that leadership is not just about restoring operations quickly, but about safeguarding the future.

However, none of this works unless you understand the ground reality. It's one thing to have a strategic vision, another to know what's actually happening at the frontlines. If you're disconnected from the user experience, your decisions, no matter how well-intentioned, will miss the mark. I made it a point to meet customers, observe their workflows, and listen to their frustrations firsthand. Numbers on a dashboard can hide a lot; a five-minute conversation with a user can reveal what really matters. I've always valued truth, the raw, unfiltered version you only get by stepping into the user's world.

COVID tested all these leadership muscles at once. Pre-pandemic, our team size was around 75. Attrition during the early months brought it down to 40–45. As the market stabilized and hiring picked up, we scaled aggressively to 175. But here's the twist: this wasn't in an office. This was full work-from-home. Leading 175 people remotely is a different kind of challenge, not necessarily harder in every way, but different enough to force new systems. In person, you can sense issues in the air, energy levels, small misunderstandings, and even subtle team dynamics. Remotely, you lose that radar. Delegation becomes both more necessary and more dangerous if you don't build control processes. I learned that in distributed setups, reporting mechanisms must be airtight, dashboards, structured updates, and defined checkpoints keep you connected to the flow of work without micromanaging. Without this structure, you drift from awareness to assumption.

With a large remote team, the balance between task management and people management becomes sharper. A manager focuses on the "what" of work; a leader focuses equally on the "who." People don't work for companies; they work for leaders. That connection is even harder to maintain without physical proximity. You have to project presence intentionally: regular check-ins, open-door policies (even if virtual), and showing up in their moments of need. It's not about knowing every answer, it's about being the person they trust will help find it.

Structure becomes your best friend when a team crosses 50–60 members. Up to that point, you can lead through direct influence and occasional ad-hoc fixes. Beyond it, you need formal escalation paths, clear role definitions, and review cadences. And you need strong middle managers. If leadership were an engine, middle managers are the pistons; without them, nothing moves efficiently. I invested in grooming them to think beyond tasks: strategic communication, people development, and upward management. Weak middle managers become choke points; strong ones are multipliers.

Scaling, I discovered, is not about headcount; it's about capability. You can't carry a large team alone. You need to spot high-potential (hi-pot) employees early, the ones who can shoulder more responsibility and move faster. Every team has a mix, hi-pots, solid contributors, and those who need more guidance. The trick is to leverage the hi-pots without burning them out, give them visibility, accelerated growth, and challenges that stretch them. Looking back, even when I identified them, I sometimes feel I could have pushed more responsibility their way. In large teams, your effectiveness is measured by how well your hi-pots lift the collective performance.

Culture is another invisible force that shapes performance. You don't "announce" culture; you live it in every interaction. It's in how you handle one-on-ones, how you conduct RCAs, how you react to mistakes. Every moment is a culture-setting moment.

Teams watch leaders closely, absorbing not just what you decide but how you decide. And this behavior trickles down; it shapes how they act when you're not in the room. I've often contrasted the cultures at Tata, Airtel, and Reliance, distinct identities shaped entirely by leadership style, flowing from the top to every level. Predictability plays a big role here, too. A team that knows how you'll react can align faster because they're not operating in fear or guesswork.

Communication in large teams has to be deliberate and often overdone. You can't assume that one email or one meeting will align everyone. Messages need to be repeated across forums, formats, and contexts. I learned this from my own leaders: consistency is key. Even your silence communicates something, so be intentional about what gets said and how often. Visuals, examples, and stories all help embed the message. And here's the rule I follow: if you think you've communicated enough, you probably haven't.

Recognition is perhaps the most cost-effective retention strategy in existence. In corporate life, visibility and acknowledgment are powerful motivators. I made recognition a habit, publicly celebrating wins, allowing individuals to present their work to senior leadership, and appreciating effort even when outcomes fell short. This last point is critical. Recognizing a failed but honest attempt removes the fear of failure and encourages innovation. In large teams, you can't possibly know every undercurrent of dissatisfaction, but you can create a culture where people feel seen. That alone can keep attrition at bay.

Staying connected personally, even in a large setup, is hard but worth the effort. I once calculated that with 175 people, if I connected with just 2–3 individuals a day, I could speak to everyone once a quarter. In the digital age, even a short WhatsApp chat makes a difference. People feel valued when their leader takes time for them; it's as much about the gesture as the content of the conversation.

Lastly, empathy has to be the constant thread. High-paced environments can make decisions feel mechanical, but behind every missed target or bug is a human being. I learned to be hard on problems but soft on people. Mistakes happen; what matters is how you treat the person who made them. See them as human beings first, not "resources." When you treat people as humans, with context, compassion, and care, you don't just earn their compliance; you earn their trust and loyalty. That's the real magic of leadership, and without it, every other system or strategy eventually falls flat.

That is what I feel, and I feel that this sense of clarity in my mind is what made me stable even as everything around me was changing. When I left IndiaMART, I felt like I was in a space with no marked walls and no charted corridors, and no preset boundaries. It was a large open field, and I was free to move whichever way. It felt marvelous at the beginning, like I did not have anything heavy on my shoulders. However, it was when I realized that with this kind of freedom also comes mutual responsibility in choosing what to do, where to go, and most so, what not to do. That is where my input-oriented thinking saved me. I did not wake up every morning thinking, "What amount of money will I make today? " Instead, my mind used to say, "What will I do today that will add value to someone, somewhere?" That automatically made my days fulfilling.

I had some days when my schedule was full of coaching calls, advisory calls, and meetings, and then there were days when I simply spent hours reading, thinking, or taking notes on ideas that may or may not ever see the light of day.". But I never felt that these were lost days because each interaction, each page I read, each self-brainstorm was piling up on my experience bank. Another major change I observed in myself during this time was that I began to appreciate the quality of conversations more than the amount of work that I had done. In the business world, once, productivity had always meant how much you could do on a single day-the number of emails answered, meetings attended, deadlines met. However, there is one time in the recent past today when I was satisfied after one simple, genuine interaction with a coaching client, more than when I had a completely hectic day filled with tick-tock duties.

Something seemed to have changed in the meaning of productivity to me. That is when I realized that not working differently but living differently is the phase in life. The relationships that I had developed throughout the years were showing their real value at this moment. Having a title or a large number of people in my team was not the reason people remembered me, but how I had touched them at the moment we worked together or talked. There were those who called to offer advice, those who called to just enquire on how I was doing, and others who called to offer opportunities. I began to realize that true networking is not about collecting visiting cards or connecting with people on LinkedIn, it's about people connection.

It's about showing up for someone when they need a sounding board, not when they can give you something. Most of the coaching work I received during this time was from individuals I hadn't heard from in years, but still felt comfortable enough with me to share their issues. Naturally, there were also doubting moments. Experimenting is not a walk in the park. Not every day is sunny. There were days I'd wake up and question whether I was making a mistake. Was I spending too much time on building a business and not enough on coaching, advising, and experimenting? Was I diluting myself too much? But then I would catch myself and tell myself that this was precisely what I had intended to do, to try, to experiment, to learn. I wasn't seeking a specific outcome.

I was creating a life in which my career brought me happiness, in which I got to make a difference in people's lives, and yet could still spend time with my family. That reminder would ground me, and I would resume my day with renewed energy. One of the unexpected byproducts of this time was how much my spiritual side started to flourish. Re-reading the Bhagavad Gita, but now with the life experience that I had accumulated, I was reading an entirely different book. Before, I had read it like a student attempting to decipher the meaning of each verse. Now, I was reading it like a person who lived some of those facts. Ideas such as detachment from results, being centered in one's duty, and equanimity amidst success and failure weren't philosophical words anymore; they were my life.

I could look back at every stage of my life, be it a career flop or an out-of-the-blue opportunity, and realize that it had been training me to live this way. It provided me with a greater sense of calm, and even in times of doubt, I never felt restless. I also began paying greater heed to my health and physical fitness during this period. In the corporate hustle, health tended to take a backseat, something to be taken care of when it began to send out warning signals. Now, I ensure that I include regular walking, easy exercise, and conscious eating. It wasn't about being on a tight regimen, but about creating habits that I could maintain.

I knew that in order to coach others well, I had to be at my physical and mental peak. People don't come to a coach for solutions so much as they do for energy, for a certain presence that gives them confidence, and I wanted to be able to provide that day in and day out. Gradually, I noticed trends in the types of coaching cases that came to me. Most were high-level leaders navigating transitions, stepping into a larger role, facing a crisis, or seeking purpose beyond professional achievement. Others were young professionals working through confidence or clarity. The genius of coaching is that no two sessions are ever identical, even if the themes repeat themselves. Every individual's path is different, and my responsibility is to accompany them, asking the questions, listening without judgment, and assisting them to discover their own solutions.

This strengthened my conviction that coaching is not about advice; it's about providing a situation where the other individual is able to think for themselves. And when they do get to their own "aha" moment, the transformation is permanent. Financially, the situation was settling down better than I had anticipated. The technology advisory projects, which were supposed to be one-offs, turned out to be a steady stream of work. They did not just keep the revenues coming in but also enabled me to remain attached to the world of technology without having to commit to any one organisation.

It was the ideal combination, leveraging my previous experience to tackle present challenges but still having the ability to follow my passion for coaching. In a large sense, this combination of technology advisory and coaching was like the sweet spot I hadn't realized I was seeking. I also realized that my approach towards opportunities had become more aware. Before, I would have jumped at anything that looked stimulating or lucrative.

Now, I asked myself one basic question before saying yes: "Will this benefit me or someone else in some way that serves my purpose?" If the response was no, then I said no politely, regardless of how enticing the opportunity appeared. This change rescued me from overextension and ensured that the work I did was significant. Volunteering remained a vital element in my life during this time. Whether it was the yearly distribution in my community or mentoring someone on an informal basis, I attempted to ensure that I was giving back beyond my immediate working circle.

The joy of knowing that someone is gaining from your time or resources cannot be beat.

It's not a matter of size; even tiny acts of kindness can make waves. On some occasions, all you need to do for someone is sit down and listen to them without criticizing them and cutting them off, without letting them know that you care and love them. Reflectively, I believe this time was one of the biggest lessons both about life and myself that any job or role has ever been. It allowed me to be comfortable with not knowing things, made me aware of what I am good at, and showed me that I did not need big stages and big groups of people to make a difference. And many times it is in the moments of sitting down, one-on-one, in the little consistent acts, in the ways you make someone feel listened to and noticed. There is a sort of quiet confidence that is there, the confidence that there is no particular mould, you can break your own mould and succeed in your choices, you can. I am no longer doing a designation or a corner office today. I am working on something meaningful, transparent relationships, and personal growth.

The best of it is, however, that I am confident this journey is but begun. There are still things to attempt, individuals to encounter, books to be read, and objectives to reframe. The field is still level, the potential is still boundless, and I'm moving forward with curiosity and belief, understanding that as long as I maintain my eye on the inputs, the outcomes will shape themselves.

Over the last twelve months, since leaving IndiaMART on 3rd May 2024, I've had the privilege of watching my own thinking evolve in ways I couldn't have imagined earlier. If I were to distill all of it, the first big learning is the importance of defining goals before taking any step. I can't stress enough how much clarity reduces mental clutter. When you know exactly what you're working towards, the day-to-day confusion of "Am I on the right track?" disappears. That constant second-guessing drains energy, and once it's gone, you feel lighter, freer, more focused. The simple act of sitting down, asking yourself the hard questions, maybe even going through coaching sessions before starting something new, is not a waste of time; it's the very foundation. Coaching isn't about someone telling you what to do; it's about someone helping you hear your own voice clearly. That's been learning number one: know your goals, explore yourself before starting, so your journey begins with intention, not accident.

The second learning has been about relationships and networking. In a secure corporate role, it's easy to underestimate them because the system carries you forward whether you nurture those bonds or not. I was guilty of that. Before leaving IndiaMART, I didn't fully grasp the depth of this truth. Only after stepping out did, I realise that relationships are not just optional extras, they're lifelines. The fact that I had, unknowingly, built good relationships in the past became one of my greatest blessings after I left. People took my calls, offered guidance, and made introductions, and all of that was possible only because seeds had been planted years ago, without any expectation.

The third learning, and one that has completely changed my perspective, is that sales is always a service. For years, I saw sales as something transactional, something that inevitably made you feel you were chasing people for your own benefit. But the truth is, if you're genuinely offering something that can help another person, following up with them is not for your benefit alone; it's for theirs. If you shift the lens from "I need this sale" to "I need to get this solution to them," your energy changes. You stop feeling guilty about persistence. Sales becomes a form of impact delivery.

Then comes the fourth learning: knowing your strengths is a superpower. I've always had an affinity for technology, but I didn't fully realise its potential until recently. Once I acknowledged it, I could see how it could be used to genuinely help people, solve problems, and contribute meaningfully. Strengths like mentoring and coaching also became clearer over time. Recognising them has allowed me to play to them, instead of trying to fit myself into spaces where I would always be average.

The fifth learning is about making every single day meaningful. There's no glory in being "busy" if nothing valuable was added to your own life or to others'. Even small acts of contribution, helping a colleague, learning something new, or creating something useful, can make the day feel worthwhile. When you accumulate enough of those meaningful days, you don't just feel productive, you feel fulfilled.

When I think about where these patterns come from, I can trace so much back to my mother. I've described her before, a woman of clarity, composure, and impeccable timing. She's someone who knows when to act, when to speak, and just as importantly, when not to. She's firm when needed, but always with open ears. She doesn't react impulsively; she responds after thought. And I see so much of that in myself now.

She never taught me these traits by lecture; it was all "life learning" through observation. I saw how she made decisions without haste, how she balanced discipline with warmth, how she reprimanded just enough to correct but never enough to create distance. She treated everyone, family or stranger, with the same respect. That respect cost her nothing but gave her everything: trust, cooperation, and goodwill. I've seen it play out in my own life exactly the same way.

Empathy is another trait that comes directly from her influence. Not sympathy, which often creates a sense of hierarchy, but empathy, the act of truly seeing from another's perspective. When you combine empathy with respect, people don't just work with you; they want to. There's no need for constant instructions or control; things get done because trust exists.

She also showed me the power of restraint. Not every situation requires your voice or your involvement. She could watch events unfold, assess the dynamics, and choose not to intervene if it wouldn't help. That ability to refrain, to not add fuel where none is needed, is something I consciously practise now. And one of her strongest lessons was never to regret a decision once it's made. Decide after due thought, and then own it fully.

When I combine my mother's influence with my own experiences, I can see the core values that have guided me all along, whether I realised it or not. The first is integrity, honesty in both ownership of success and in acknowledging the contributions of others. The second is respect, for everyone, regardless of title or background. The third is hard work, the kind that makes "walking on one leg" look easy. The fourth is helping others whenever possible; it's not optional, it's a responsibility. The fifth is excellence through ownership. If you take something on, do it well enough to elevate both yourself and the outcome. The sixth is empathy, which builds genuine, lasting connections. And the seventh is curiosity, the drive to dig deeper into people, systems, and situations.

These values shape not just how I work but how I handle risk and failure today. In my twenties, failure felt catastrophic. It hurt my confidence and made me avoid risks. My choices then were guided by safety and social approval. I wanted to do what was "right" by collective standards, not necessarily what was right for me. Risk-taking barely existed in my vocabulary because the fear of failure was stronger than the desire for growth.

Now, the equation has flipped. I've learned that failure is not the opposite of success; it's the step that makes success possible. The analogy of falling off a cycle finally makes sense to me. It's not about enjoying the fall; it's about realising that falling is part of the learning process. Each failure carries feedback. It tells you which path won't work and pushes you to explore another.

Once you make peace with failure, you automatically become more comfortable with risk. You stop seeing it as recklessness and start seeing it as the only route to breakthroughs. Risk-taking now feels like growth in action; it's courage aligned with purpose. It's trusting your capabilities enough to say, "Even if this doesn't work, I'll learn something that will make the next step better." Without that mindset, I wouldn't have been able to leave IndiaMART in the first place. That decision was a calculated risk based on clarity, confidence, and a belief that safety is not the same as progress.

In the end, the last year has been a blend of self-awareness, inherited wisdom, and a willingness to reframe old fears. It has been about turning goals into anchors, relationships into bridges, sales into service, strengths into platforms, and values into daily practice. My mother's influence runs like a steady undercurrent through all of it, quiet but powerful, shaping my mindset in ways I sometimes notice only in hindsight. And perhaps the most important shift is that I now see failure not as a signal to stop, but as a signpost pointing towards the next opportunity. Risk is no longer something to tiptoe around; it's something to step into with open eyes and steady feet, knowing that whatever comes next, I'm building forward.

Chapter 9: Moments of Doubt vs. Moments of Triumph

If I look back over my career, I can honestly say I never really felt "low" in the way most people describe it. I had moments of stress, of course. Small dips. A bad week here, a tough month there, those natural fluctuations that are part of any professional journey. Sometimes, once or twice in a year, I'd feel a little unsettled, as if something wasn't falling into place. But then, almost without fail, things would bounce back. Targets would be met, recognition would follow, and the energy would return. Those little blips didn't trouble me much. They were just weather changes on an otherwise clear road.

But there was a particular phase, one that stretched across months, when the feeling was different. It wasn't just a temporary cloud passing overhead. It was quieter, deeper, and harder to name. By every external measure, I was doing exceptionally well. In fact, I was at one of the highest points of my corporate career. I had joined IndiaMART in December 2010 as an Assistant Product Manager, and over the years, had risen to the position of Chief Information Officer. I'd been invited to join the board as a CXO, worked directly with the CEO, navigated critical decisions during the COVID years, and led large, complex teams. From the outside, it was the picture of success.

Now, never mind the inside is wrong somewhere. Not that I was unhappy, manically crying and crashing about--but the gradual fading out of a light which had previously been so bright. The enthusiasm that I had borne for so many years, the stimulus which had formerly made me bound into every new enterprise, had now vanished. I was doing well, crossing all the aspects of being a good employee and producing results... but still, I felt disconnected from my own work. It was a role with prestige, but a significant responsibility, and my internal alignment was sliding.

Admitting this is not so easy when you are performing successfully on paper. At gatherings, at conferences, at business functions, I still appeared as the esteemed, successful leader I had always been. And in the middle of all that, I had been asking myself the somewhat uncomfortable questions: Is this the life that I truly want? Or just the one I was trained to chase? And if it's not exactly what I want, do I have the courage to change it? Or am I going to keep moving forward because that's the "safe" thing to do?

It wasn't burnout in the typical sense. I could still perform at a high level, still deliver on my responsibilities. But I was exhausted; it felt like I was running on reserves. Every decision, every initiative, took a little more effort than it once had. The joy I used to feel when building new products or solving difficult problems had dulled. And I knew enough about myself to recognise that if I didn't act, the erosion would continue.

That's when the idea of doing my own startup began to take shape. I had spent years immersed in product, technology, and business. I understood markets, teams, execution, and scale. I felt, at least from a capability perspective, that I was ready to build something from scratch. So I did what felt right: I went to my CEO and told him I wanted to do something of my own.

At that time, I had no clear plan. No defined product, no business model, not even a specific industry in mind. I only had the conviction that I wanted to create. Unsurprisingly, he wasn't eager to let me go. We had a close working relationship, and he had been more than a boss; he was a mentor and, in many ways, a guardian figure in my corporate life. I'd learned an immense amount from him over the years. We spoke openly, and after some discussion with him, with other senior leaders, and even with my executive coach at IndiaMART, I decided to stay for a while longer.

A year later, I finally had something tangible. I had done some market research, built an early prototype, run through potential business models, and identified the opportunity I wanted to pursue. This time, when I went to my CEO, my pitch was much more concrete. After a lot of persuasion, truly, a lot, he agreed that I could start transitioning out, provided we found someone to take over my role. He even suggested a hybrid approach: I could work on my startup for three months while continuing in my CIO capacity, and if it gained traction, I could then make the leap.

I took the offer. For those three months, I lived in two worlds: corporate leadership during the day, startup exploration in every spare hour. And in those hours, reality hit me. Building a startup wasn't just about passion and ideas; it was 24×7 commitment, with no safety net. I had two young children, and I could see the strain it would place on my family. As much as I believed in the dream, I realised the timing wasn't right. And so, I stayed. Again.

But the original problem hadn't gone away. The same disconnection, the same quiet fading of enthusiasm, was still there. I found myself asking a new question: If not a startup, then what? Because I knew one thing for sure, continuing exactly as I was, for the rest of my life, was not the answer.

That's when coaching entered my life. I signed up for coach training, not as a career move at first, but as a way to pause and reflect. In the very first three days of training, I stopped running. I slowed down. I journaled, I read, I asked myself questions I'd been avoiding. Two months later, there was another three-day session. And by the time I had completed the program and started doing peer coaching sessions, the real breakthroughs began to happen.

For the first time in years, I was looking inward with complete honesty. I realised that the courage I had been reserving for "someday" needed to be used now. I chose to pursue a different path, not because my corporate career was failing, but because my alignment was. And I knew alignment mattered more than safety. Safety might protect you, but it doesn't fulfil you.

I worked on my support system. I leaned on my family, my mentors, and a few close friends. There were moments when my own confidence wavered, but theirs didn't. Their belief in me helped me believe in myself again.

When I began coaching, I felt something click into place. This was work that energised me, helping people grow, creating possibilities, building new paths. It was different from the adrenaline of corporate achievements, but in a way, it felt richer. Advisory work followed naturally because of my technology and leadership background. I realised that advising was just another form of helping, another way of serving the purpose I had rediscovered.

I didn't try to rebuild my life in one leap. I took it one clear action at a time. Each step forward created enough momentum for the next. And slowly, that quiet low I had experienced for so long began to lift.

Fifteen months after leaving my role, I can say I'm in a good place, not because of monetary gains (those were never my primary reason for leaving) but because I'm finally living in alignment with my own purpose. My coaching and advisory work is not just my job anymore; it is who I am and about what I believe in.

The only thing that I learn about that time is that sometimes hitting your rock bottom is where you get the launchpad to your greatest change. However, it requires you to have the guts to listen to yourself, think unfettered, and after that, do so.

A lot of my happiness before was connected with corporate achievements to a staggering degree: projects completed, KPIs met, promotions gained. There is one that seems to shine the brightest: that is April 2018, when my CEO called me out of nowhere and inquired whether I could maybe accompany him to the airport. I just heard the god talking, and I responded Yes. On the drive, he told me they had been searching for a CIO for some time, but hadn't found the right person. They needed someone who understood product and technology, not just IT systems. And he offered me the role.

That moment meant a lot. It wasn't just a title; it was the recognition of years of hard work, commitment, and trust. On the surface, my expression stayed composed, but inside, I was deeply moved. It felt like the culmination of a decade-long journey, and at the same time, the beginning of another.

You don't get offered a CXO role just because you delivered a single project well or achieved one big result. Those things help, but they're only chapters in a much longer book. The real reason someone entrusts you with such responsibility is because of years, sometimes decades, of showing up with commitment, resilience, and consistency. Looking back, I think that's what he had seen in me over the years. Until then, my career had followed a steady path. I had received promotions, led larger teams, and taken on broader responsibilities. Every step felt earned, but they were still steps in the same direction. This time, it was different. This time, the shift was seismic.

It wasn't just the title that changed; it was the function, the scope, and the proximity to the very heart of the company's leadership. I wasn't moving from Head of Product to Chief Product Officer. I was being asked to step into the role of Chief Information Officer. That meant moving out of my familiar terrain and into an entirely different function, one that was closer to him, closer to the CEO, and closer to the company's core strategic decision-making. It was a big thing for me, especially because in my career until then, I had never switched titles into something completely different.

If I look back at why it happened, I believe the common thread is that I had always focused on solving real business problems. Not just doing my job, but going after the root cause, creating solutions that mattered, and then rallying people around them. Over the years, I had built high-performing teams, delivered outcomes with ownership, and upheld integrity even when it was inconvenient. And in the culture of our organization, those weren't just good traits, they were core values: teamwork, responsibility, integrity, passion. I had internalized them deeply, and without realizing it, I was living them every day. So, when this role came my way, I saw it as more than a job offer. It was recognition of all those invisible years of effort.

For me, the meaning came in layers. First, it was validation. It told me that leadership trusted not only my skills, but also my judgment and my ability to align technology with the company's long-term strategy. I've never seen myself purely as a technical person or purely as a business person. My strength was always in being the bridge; I understood the business, I understood the product, and I understood technology. That combination meant I could see how technology decisions shaped business outcomes, and vice versa. And when you can align technology with strategy, you can drive change across the organization with clarity, even in complexity.

The second layer was consistency. Consistency matters more than we often admit. We love stories of overnight success, but in reality, growth is quiet, steady, and often unnoticed. My journey had been exactly that. From being hands-on in execution to designing long-term roadmaps, from delivering small wins to influencing decisions at the highest levels, I had grown one deliberate step at a time. This role made that growth visible, but the truth is, it had been happening silently for years.

The third layer was personal meaning. I come from a background where nothing was handed to me. Every step I took was earned with effort, persistence, and sometimes sacrifice. That's why this moment felt different; it wasn't just a professional milestone, it was a personal one. It reminded me of nights like 2nd December 2011, my first wedding anniversary, when I had guests at home, my in-laws visiting, and the evening was meant to be about celebration. Instead, a critical technical issue emerged on one of the products I was responsible for. From 7 p.m. that evening until 9 a.m. the next morning, I was working with the office team to resolve it. That's the kind of commitment that doesn't show up in a résumé, but it's the kind that builds trust over the years.

And finally, the fourth layer changed how I saw myself. I'll be honest, before this, I never fully understood what a CIO role truly meant. But the moment you hear "CXO," you know it comes with proximity to the CEO, involvement in defining the company's direction, and the responsibility of influencing business priorities at the highest level. It's not just about delivering results, it's about shaping them. That realization filled me with both pride and humility.

That day also reaffirmed something I've come to believe deeply: when you consistently lead with honesty, work ethic, empathy, and ownership, the universe notices, even if you're not making noise about it. That's why this moment remains my proudest. Not just because of the role, but because of what it represented about the journey that got me there.

And yet, there's another reason this moment is so meaningful to me; it's tied to a realization that came much later. A former team member, someone I had mentored years earlier at IndiaMART, reached out unexpectedly. He said, "I just wanted to tell you that the way you led us back then changed how I approach leadership today." He went on to describe moments I had almost forgotten, projects under extreme pressure, deadlines that seemed impossible, and a climate of uncertainty. He said he remembered how I stayed calm, how I took responsibility without shifting blame, how I stood in front of the team when things went wrong but stepped back to give them credit when things went right.

What struck me was that I never realized I was being watched so closely at the time. To me, I was just doing what felt right, protecting my team, communicating openly, and making sure people felt supported. I wasn't performing leadership; I was just living it. But to him, those moments became a reference point for what leadership should look like.

It wasn't the first time I had heard something like this. In 2017 or 2018, within the organization itself, someone had told me a similar story. They described events from 2014 or 2015, when I had been handling a sudden surge in responsibilities. They, too, had observed and learned from how I navigated those times. These conversations taught me something important: you don't always know who you're inspiring. Sometimes, just being yourself is the most powerful thing you can do. You don't need to copy anyone else's style or pretend to be someone you're not. Authenticity has its own gravity.

The second lesson was that real impact often happens quietly. It's not about the speeches you make or the slogans you repeat; it's about the actions you take when no one's taking notes. People don't follow what you say; they follow what you do. Just like children learn more from what they see than from what they're told, adults in the workplace are no different. Your actions are your true message.

The third lesson was about meaning. Our careers are often measured by achievements, promotions, revenue growth, and successful launches. But the deeper meaning of a journey comes from how you make others feel along the way. Achievements are important, but the imprint you leave on people's lives often lasts longer than any corporate milestone.

Hearing those words from my former team member moved something inside me. It reminded me that leadership is less about standing in the spotlight and more about leaving a light for others to follow. Even today, more than sixteen years into my career, I still get messages from people I've worked with in the past. Some recall specific projects; others remember small acts of support I barely noticed at the time. But almost all of them tell me they were inspired during those times. And that, more than anything, is what I carry forward.

Chapter 10: Advice for the Young Dreamers

When you find yourself at a crossroads and you do not know whether what you will do next will take you nearer to your dreams or yet to another dead-end street, you may find yourself thinking that the world has hit its pause button on your life. You watch others progress, prosper, meet milestones, and all you seem to do is walk in a circle. I do want you to remember, at such times, that this is not an emotion peculiar to you; at these moments, it is an emotion that I also myself have persuaded myself, after forty years of witnessing careers rise, and fall, and begin again, and seize upon their careers once more: I also, when these things happen to me, cannot believe that it is a unique emotion.

You are not the only person who has ever gotten lost, and you will not be the last. Rather, you are in an excellent company, because every single person you idolise (every global leader, every successful entrepreneur, every famous artist, or every senior in your own company) has at one point or another, woken and wondered whether he or she was travelling in the right direction. It is not a defect; it just means that you are alive and learning and thinking.

Being in a place of stuck is not that you are a failure, but that you are growing. It is the feeling that screams at you that you are not on autopilot at all, that you are unsure where you are and where to. The wonder, the sadness, though, is a sign of depth. Most individuals move through life without ever stopping to pose themselves tough questions. The fact that you even know you are stuck is already ahead of others who never take the time to think.

Awareness, however, won't carry you forward; you must take action. Which leads to the second truth: clarity arises through action, not thought. Too much, we get mired in our own minds, running through scenarios, weighing risks, waiting for the ideal plan to emerge before taking action. But life does not often repay the thinker; it pays the doer. When you're feeling lost, take small steps. Do something new. Volunteer for a project with which you're completely unfamiliar. Take a workshop on a skill only loosely related to your present position. Contact someone whose career trajectory fascinates you and ask them how they got started. Every step, no matter how small, is a vote for progress.

Even if the action you take today doesn't directly result in your long-term dream, it will bring you knowledge, experience, and contacts that you didn't possess yesterday. And those, gradually, make up the map that overthinking could never provide. When I reflect on the instances that altered the direction of my career, nearly none of them originated from being in isolation, attempting to solve everything out. They arrived at saying yes to possibilities ahead of time when I wasn't ready yet, at stepping out even when I did not know where I was headed.

The third truth is one more young professionals should learn early: your value is not attached to a title or a timeline. I've watched geniuses hold themselves back because they were too focused on comparing themselves to others, holding their progress up against someone else's Instagram highlight reel,

LinkedIn posts, or professional title. But life isn't a competition, and careers aren't synchronized swimming. We all develop at our own speed. You might be 25 and still figuring things out, but your friend has already started a startup. That doesn't make you behind; it makes you unique. And unique is not a defect. There isn't a master calendar that dictates you have to accomplish X by age Y. Some people peak in their twenties, others in their fifties, and many peak multiple times in various ways. Concentrate on your improvement, not perfection. Ask yourself continuously, "Am I progressing, even if it's slowly? Comparison game is not only useless; it's distracting from the work that truly matters, to your own path. Perfection is never the goal; progress is. And the glory of progress is that it compounds. One small, less-than-perfect step today can result in an enormous, life-altering opportunity tomorrow.

The fourth truth is one I learned both the easy way and the hard way: "seek help.". The myth of the self-made individual is just that, a myth. Every individual who has done something remarkable has been lifted, guided, or pushed by another individual at some stage. There is no demigod who climbs to the summit of their mountain in solitude without resting on the shoulder of another human being. And yet we are reluctant to reach out. We're afraid of coming across as weak, or being judged, or hearing the word "no." But the truth is: people are much more likely to help you than you realize, and many times they're happy to do so because they've been right where you are. They understand what it's like to be stuck, uncertain, and looking for the next handhold. And they recall the individual who reached out to them when they needed it most. That's why they'll offer you one. Ask your mentors. Ask your co-workers. Ask your friends. And if you can't think of anyone in your immediate network, broaden your network. Go to events. Join online forums. Approach people whose work interests you. You'll be amazed at how many doors will open when you just knock. The secret is to be authentic, don't just ask a favor, ask for direction, insight, and learning.

When I revisit the mentors who changed my life drastically, in most cases, we started the relationship with a simple, honest question: Can I ask you anything? That single question has given rise to opportunities, clarity, and progress that I would never have been able to engineer myself.

The fifth truth and most desirable, perhaps, is to develop belief as a habit. There are innumerable people in this world who did not quit due to a lack of talent and opportunity, but they just quit due to a loss of belief in themselves, even before the results may have shown. Belief is your silent engine, which keeps moving when nothing appears to be working in your present. And faith doesn't equal arrogance or blind hoping; it means having faith in your potential when it's not yet manifest to anyone else, least of all, yourself. Potential is not necessarily quantifiable in its early development. You may not have results yet, but that doesn't mean the potential is absent; it just means it hasn't yet reached its full surface. And yes, outcomes will ultimately demonstrate your ability, but you require faith in order to reach the point where outcomes can even occur. Faith is what allows you to remain in the game long enough for the scoreboard to pick up on your effort. Confidence isn't about knowing all of the answers initially; it's about believing in yourself to work them out along the way. Trust that your unique combination of experiences, skills, and perspectives has value.

Just have faith, and things will surely be in place one step at a time. And best of all, believe that you are doing what you should be doing even when it doesn't feel like it. When I combine all these five truths, I know I am not alone, I must act, not think or fall into the trap of thought, repudiate timelines and titles as a means of determining personal value, seek help, and develop the lean to believe. I think it's all more than just survival advice in a bad situation. In many ways, they are the building blocks of a complete, happy career and life. I have suffered moments when I had doubts about each decision, when I was in doubt about whether I was appropriate for the course that I had chosen. But each time when I returned to these ideals, I discovered my way forward--not in a straight flight, but in a procession made up of little, resolute steps. In case you have lost track of the reading, here is what you should understand: you do not need to have everything figured out. You simply need to keep going, keep learning, keep asking, and keep believing. The soft voice within you that whispers, "There's more for me," is not deceiving you. It is your compass. Follow it. The road will make itself known as you travel it.

Discuss it with one or two trusted minds. Not everybody, as too many might contribute to the confusion. But I have found that when I discuss my dilemma with one or two people I trust deeply, mentors, colleagues, friends, they bring perspective I may not have seen in the moment. It's not about dumping the burden of the decision, but about seeing things through different eyes. Sometimes, a single sentence from them can help me see a path that was invisible to me before. And many times, I have realized that when I speak about my challenge out loud, I end up hearing my own thoughts in a clearer way. It's almost as if the act of explaining the situation to someone else forces my brain to organize the mess in my head. That organization alone tends to make the way ahead clearer. But this will only work if you are truthful with the people you speak to, no withholding of details, no coloring the picture brighter or more dismal than it actually is. Present it as it is, even though it's uncomfortable, because only that way will you receive feedback that counts.

The sixth principle is, resolve, and then commit to it wholeheartedly. I've learned that indecision can be more dangerous than a bad decision. Pressure situations have a clock running in the background, and the more time you waste, the greater the pressure. After you've assembled your facts, consulted your values, zoomed in and out, distinguished between fear and fact, and sought the counsel of wise minds, you must commit. Make the decision, then give it your full weight. Own the result, good or ill, and ride it out. That is where leadership is truly tested, not in being decisive per se, but in holding to it, particularly when others are questioning you. There is no such thing as a perfect pressure decision. All choices involve trade-offs. But what separates somebody who freezes and somebody who rises above in these moments is the courage to move forward with uncertainty.

And here's the thing I have seen repeatedly: pressure reveals character. It strips away the layers we wear every day and shows us, and everyone around us, who we really are. If you lose your temper under pressure, people will remember that. If you stay composed and act with integrity, people will remember that too. In a lot of cases, every difficult choice is a chance to reinforce the trust people have in you or to undermine it. That's why reverting back to values matters; it keeps you grounded when the tempest attempts to destabilize you.

I recall one time a few years ago when we were releasing a pivotal product update. We were on the verge of making a public promise we had given, the campaigns were already up, and then it was discovered that there was a huge flaw in the system. The business side wanted to push on, because it could be hacked afterwards. The technical team insisted that this would make a big mess for customers. Time was running out, and both parties looked to me. At that point, I panned out, what's more important, making the date or honoring our commitment to quality to customers? To me, quality had never been a negotiable principle. So I made the call to postpone the launch. It wasn't an easy call; it was additional cost, some short-term reputational loss, and a lot of awkward conversations. But in the long term, it reinforced the customer trust that we had established over the years. I still hear people say today that they admired that decision because it was customer-first. That's the long-term effect I refer to.

Pressure moments also teach you humility. There have been instances where I made an incorrect decision. Yes, even after all the models and all the thought processes, I've been incorrect. At those moments, what preserved my integrity was not faking that the error did not occur, but taking responsibility publicly. I recall saying to my staff, "This one's on me. I made the call, and I underestimated." That vulnerability doesn't make you lose standing; it really makes your standing stronger because individuals can see that you are human and responsible. It makes them feel confident that even if you do something else stupid in the future, you will take responsibility for it and correct it, rather than cover it up.

Pressure is like a muscle over the years: you can condition it. The first time you encounter a high-pressure choice, your body and your head will respond with panic. But the more you experience such moments and deal with them consciously, the more you become skilled at dealing with that initial surge of fear and adrenaline. You figure out how to slow your breathing, slow your thinking, and remind yourself: I have been here before. I've survived before. That reminder to yourself is so strong because it immediately knocks down the sense that this is the "end of the world." It's never the end of the world. Even the largest catastrophes you can imagine, leave them alone for a while, and they give way to just another chapter in your book.

Another lesson I've learned is that pressure decisions are not often solely about the decision in and of themselves; they're also about guiding the people through it. If you get the decision right but make your team feel abandoned or unheard in doing so, you lose their trust. If you make a hard decision and take time to tell them why, include them in the thought process, and demonstrate that you paid attention to their viewpoint, even if they don't agree, they are much more likely to back you. Individuals can accept something that they don't want; what they cannot accept is being disrespected or dismissed.

I believe that the reason so many leaders blow it under pressure is not that they make the wrong decision, but that they don't take the emotional management aspect of the job seriously enough. In high-pressure situations, others are not only looking to you for the solution, they're also looking to you to set the tone. If you stay calm, they will find a way to stay calm. Panic, on the other hand, is contagious. This is why fact and fear separation is so important; you can't be the calm eye of the storm if you are being dragged around by fear as well.

One of the best things I habituated myself into is to pause before responding. It sounds easy, but it is more difficult than it seems. When an urgent email comes in, when someone brings bad news, when a crisis hits, the natural reaction is to respond immediately. But I've trained myself to take a beat. Even if it's just 60 seconds of deep breathing, that pause can mean the difference between a reactive decision and a thoughtful one. During that delay, I recall my values, the larger context, and the necessity to act rather than react. I don't know how many times the little lag has prevented me from speaking words I would regret or hasty action not well considered.

Ultimately, making difficult choices in high-pressure situations boils down to preparation combined with attitude. The preparation is developing those habits, checking your values, zooming in and out, distinguishing fact from fear, having trusted advisors, and being decisive. The mindset is embracing that there is no perfect decision. You will get things wrong. Some calls will bug you for a period. But as long as your compass is set on integrity, ownership, and lasting effect, you will discover that your decisions will generally stand the test of time.

And here's the reassuring bit: pressure moments are fleeting. They seem crushing while you're in them, but they go away. What will last is not the moment itself, but the reputation you create from it. Years down the line, folks will hardly recall the specific issue, but they will recall how you appeared, how you behaved toward them, and if you were for something or merely went with the flow. I've witnessed this time and again, both personally and in others' lives, your conduct during the most difficult 5% of the moments determines how others perceive you in the other 95%.

So when you're in that next pressure moment, remember: this is a gift. Not only an impediment, not only a challenge, but a possibility to deepen your own leadership muscle, to establish trust, and to show what you're really about. That change, from "why is this happening to me" to "how can I grow through this", is the most powerful change you can make. It doesn't make the situation easier, but it changes how you experience it. And in the long run, that makes all the difference.

Because, ultimately, pressure is unavoidable. You can't help but have it if you care about doing real work. The issue isn't "how do I get around pressure," but "how do I conduct myself despite it so that I emerge better, with my principles preserved, and the people around me trusting me more." That, to me, is the true test of making the correct choice in times of pressure.

I have long felt that ownership isn't so much about doing your job right, that is, your job as assigned, it's about loving the outcome as if you were the sole responsibility for it. That changes everything. When you work for showing up, you just show up and put in time; when you work with ownership, you put yourself in. And the people around you take notice, even when you think nobody is watching. My own professional life is riddled with instances where a subtle choice to take responsibility, doing something without being asked, staying late to work on an emergency problem, assisting someone on another team, came back to pay me in ways I never could have imagined. The anecdote I mentioned before, when my boss raised my pay when I didn't even expect it, is evidence of that. He had to see my work over the months, not in the big one-time thing, but in the small, steady acts of owning it outside my job description. Ownership is a silent resume; it talks even when you are not there.

Something else I learned, and which was even more apparent to me as I transitioned between jobs, is that relationships are an unseen asset that accrues interest over time. Relationship building doesn't equate to collecting cards or connecting on LinkedIn; it's about actually investing in people. As I was preparing to leave

IndiaMART, for the past week I spent walking from floor to floor, bidding goodbye to everyone. That was when it really hit home, how many actual relationships I had formed, and how many appreciated our relationship. A few of them I had worked very closely with, the others simply greeted with a smile down the hallway, assisted with a minor problem, or chatted over tea. Those moments, as insignificant as they seemed at the time, had built up into trust and warmth. And this is the truth: your skillset may land you the job, but it's the relationships that are going to open doors you can't even imagine yet. Opportunities don't usually come through official applications; they come through dialogue, through someone remembering your name and how you treated them.

One of the most valuable tips I can share with young professionals is this: be actually interested in people. Don't network; connect. Ask questions, listen, and recall things about their lives. It's not manipulation, it's concern. People are able to sense the difference between a person who is speaking with them only because they need something from them and a person who really cares about them as an individual. And here's the amazing part: when you serve other people, when you invest in their development, you naturally develop yourself. The learning you accumulate, the insights you gather, and the credibility you build are professional assets that no economic downturn can ever take away from you.

Sure, none of this will matter if you're not always learning. The most pernicious trap that a young professional can fall into is believing that once they get a good job, the learning is over. The truth is the opposite: your actual learning begins once you're in the workforce. The skills that landed you a job may not be the skills that keep you competitive five years down the line. Technology advances, industries shift, expectations change. The only thing that keeps you one step ahead is the capacity to adapt, and flexibility is a learned trait. You need to practice learning rapidly, unlearning the old ways, and learning anew. I refer to it as "learning how to learn," and it's worth more than any one degree or credential.

Flexibility is not a matter of tools or processes; it's a state of mind. I've watched individuals push back against change merely because "this is the way we've always done things." That mindset is toxic to your career. A business will always appreciate a person who says, "I don't know that yet, but I'll learn it," more than a person who refuses to play outside of what they currently know. This is the reason why businesses recruit based on attitude rather than skill; skills can be trained, but a close-mindedness is much more difficult to alter. If you approach every project with an attitude of, "What can I learn here?

"You will always have a way to grow, even if what you are doing does not appear related to your final objectives. Critical thinking is also an underappreciated skill that comes with learning to learn. It's not sufficient to merely do the work, you have to know why you're doing it, what the larger picture is, and how your actions are part of it.". Most young professionals make the mistake of blindly executing instructions without questioning. I promote the opposite. Question procedures, offer ideas on how to improve, and consider the long-term effects of decisions. This doesn't imply you question everything your seniors tell you, but you ought to always be working actively with the work rather than just doing it like a machine.

That curiosity not only makes you more competent at your job, but it also sends the message to others that you are committed to the success of the organization, not your own success. The reality is, career advancement is not typically a linear ladder; it's a jungle gym, with lateral steps, detours not anticipated, and moments when you think you're holding on by one hand. That's why long-term careers are founded on three pillars: a learner's mindset, ownership, and relationships. Skills will shift. Industries will shift. Even your goals may shift.

But if you possess the capacity for learning, the willingness to take responsibility, and the habit of creating real relationships, you can adapt to any change. I've been asked many times, "What's the secret to remaining motivated despite adversity? " For me, it has never been about constant motivation; it's about having a platform so solid that even when I get tired or have doubts, I just keep going. When you own it, you don't give up because things become difficult. When you have relationships, you don't go through things alone.

When you have a learner's mindset, you don't view obstacles as walls but rather as puzzles to be solved. And when all three are put together, you no longer fear change and begin to view it as a chance. I'd like to tell an anecdote that brings everything together. There was a project I worked on many years ago that was well beyond my comfort zone. The deadline was tight, the stakes were high, and I had no experience with some of the tools I was being asked to use. It would have been simple to panic or hope in secret that someone else might step up. Instead, I leaned into the learning. I lingered after work to read manuals, contacted a colleague who was experienced in the field, and asked questions without fear of appearing inexperienced. I accepted the results rather than hiding behind excuses of not having experience. And I continued to check in with the people who were involved, ensuring that they felt informed and supported.

The project ultimately turned out well, not because I became an expert overnight but because I went at it with the proper mindset.

What that experience did was build my reputation in ways I couldn't have scripted, and it led to doors opening up for me in the future. In retrospect, I know that the same habits that got me through that project have gotten me through my career. The willingness to learn, the choice to step up even when it's awkward, and the work at keeping close relationships, these aren't bonus features; they're the core. They're what transform a job into a career, and a career into a legacy. To anyone who is new or stuck, I would tell this: worry less about attempting to foresee the ideal path and more about developing the characteristics that will enable you to take any path. Opportunities are not linear. Industries shift overnight.

But adaptability, the willingness to take ownership, and authenticity to care for others will never be out of fashion. These are the things that will make you not only successful, but meaningful. Ultimately, it's not about how quickly you rise or how much you make in the early years; it's about who you are in the process. Titles may disappear, companies may fold, markets may collapse, but the human you become from ongoing learning, real relationships, and real ownership will always propel you forward. And that's why, wherever I am or whatever I do next, I know I'm creating something that lasts well beyond a single job or accomplishment.

Chapter 11: Looking Inward & Looking Ahead

What should be the attitude towards vision, growth, and success in the long term? It is one of those questions that really can ring so large that people either choose not to approach them all together, or they attempt to respond to it in a very complex manner. The fun of it is, however, that to me, the thinking on vision should be as follows: begin with clarity, transform with bravery.

Most times, people anticipate that their vision should be crystal clear right from the start, as if somehow some divine script is being written for them on day one. The thing is, it never works out like that. You are not god, and you are not sure what will happen ten years later. You cannot predict all twists, all leaps of pitch, all pitfalls. Vision should not be an accurate road map; it is a sense of where you are going and getting in the direction that interests you because of the feeling of what is important. That is a good place to start.

I always tell young people who ask me about vision: don't freeze in anticipation of a perfectly articulated goal. Begin with what gets you fired up. If something feels significant, if something makes you feel alive, then let that power inform your decisions. That doesn't mean that you should lock yourself away from the unknown or pin yourself to one strict path.

In fact, it's just the opposite. Keep the doors open. Keep yourself on hand for new opportunities, new learnings, and new facts, because each new fact will introduce a new level of excitement, and each new opportunity will unlock a door you could never have dreamt of. Your experiences hone your vision over time. It sharpens as you go along, and not before you start. Most importantly, move.

I didn't know I'd become a CIO. I did not know that one day I would become a coach. I did not know that I would have so-called fast-track growth in my career. On day one of my journey, none of that was clear to me. I completed my B.Tech in Computer Science. Then I completed an MBA in finance. My initial career role was in sales at ICICI.

Did I ever think that one day I would be a product manager?

Not at all. But one step followed another. When I was working, I was inquisitive, I continued learning, I began experimenting, and the next thing I knew, I was in SEO and then product management. If you sit back and look at it today, it seems to be a linear story. But to live it then, it was all about being ready to learn and take the next step forward.

That's why I believe the secret is not having a vision perfect but having a direction rooted in your heart and the courage to course correct along the way. As new facts become available, you learn, you adapt, you re-line up. Vision is not a static thing. Vision is uncovered, experienced, and honed over time. It's a snapshot that only becomes clear as you draw nearer. That's vision, and that's what I've learned.

Now, let's discuss growth. Lots of people assume that growth is purely a matter of moving up, promotions, pay, and titles. But growth isn't all about moving up. Growth is also deep and wide. Ask yourself: am I developing not only my career, but also my character, my potential, and my capability to serve others? Am I learning? Am I pushing myself? Am I becoming a person who is capable of taking on bigger responsibilities, not only technically but also emotionally? That is true growth.

For me, growth has been about asking: Am I growing my ability to think more critically? Am I becoming more flexible? Am I learning to work more collaboratively? Am I learning how to build people around me? Those are more profound questions of growth. Because if you're just running after titles and salaries, you might grow on paper, but in your heart, you might still be. Growth means that your roots are becoming stronger. Your capacity is growing.

And then success. This is the aspect that has altered the most for me over the years. As a young fellow, success was the form of results. Success was about how much one accomplished, how quickly one accomplished it, and how public these accomplishments were made to be. It was about comparison: who's doing better, who's in front, who's quicker. But over time, success began to mean something entirely different.

Now I know that success is really about impact. It's about the person I am and how I cause others to be successful. My definition of success has changed from comparison to contribution. From speed to substance.

From noise to meaning. The most successful individuals I have encountered in my life are not those who claim the largest wins or the most finances. They are the ones who are truly at peace with their decisions. They have meaning for themselves and for others. They aren't just proud of what they've won; they are thankful for the process.

If I put this in an image, I'd say: imagine your path as planting a tree. Vision is the seed. Development is the roots and branches. And success is the shadow that you cast on others. A tree doesn't exist for itself. Its true purpose is in the shelter and the sustenance that it offers.

Likewise, true success is about the difference that you make to the lives of others. That's the sort of success that endures.

Certainly, I am still learning each and every day. One of the large lessons that I have had to learn is that I don't have to always be in charge in order to make things happen. In earlier parts of my life, I felt like if I didn't have complete control, if I didn't have all of the answers, nothing was going to happen.

But over time, what I came to understand was that this isn't actually true. You can't control everything. You can't do everything for yourself. And you don't have to. Laying off is not the same as laying down. Trusting others, trusting the process, trusting the environment, these things will usually yield better outcomes than attempting to control it all.

I have learned this through coaching in a very practical sense. There isn't a single potent question or optimal question in coaching. There isn't a rigid script. What matters is the process, being fully present before, during, and after a session, creating space for things to unfold. That's the process. And when you trust the process, magic happens.

Similarly, in life, if you trust the process, trust your people, and trust the environment, you often see better results than if you try to force control. I've experienced this in my corporate career, too. I never really dictated where my career was going. I simply went with the flow like a river. Whatever came along, I picked it up. I trusted God, I trusted the situation, and I trusted what I knew was important. If I were honest, if I was respectful, and if I worked hard, I knew nobody could deter me. That faith propelled me ahead.

Another strong lesson for me is that my energy is my best asset.

Earlier, I used to believe that time management is everything. Now I have come to understand that it's not time, it's energy that actually counts. You can have lots of time, but without energy, you won't make headway. However, when you understand what fills you with energy, what drains you, and consciously fuel your energy, nothing can hold you back; you can get ten times more done in half the time. In my own case, this change altered all. By keeping my energy in check, I am able to be a better asset to my work, to my people, and to myself.

I have also come to understand that there are so many such unseen habits in me- the old thoughts, the old tales, and at times they can be subtly insidious as they sneak their way into my judgments and responses, and I do not ever realize.

I am yet to learn how to trap them, confront them, and rewrite them. Previously, I used to think I needed all the answers. Now I understand I don't. Some of the answers come with time. Some of the answers are not for me to understand at all. I used to think I needed to be in control. Now I realize letting go sometimes makes for better results. It takes time to make these changes, but they are needed for growth.

And perhaps one of the largest discoveries for me is that there is always deeper depth to find.

Depth trumps breadth. For years, I was tempted to do more, get more spread out, take on more things. But now I have learned that real transformation is not from breadth, it is from depth. It is from coaching, leadership, relationships, or spirituality that real growth occurs when one goes deeper. More coaching sessions don't make a difference. What makes a difference is the depth of each session. More relationships don't make a difference. What matters is how deep and meaningful those relationships are. I'm still learning to go deeper rather than just wider.

And lastly, I've discovered that contentment and ambition go hand in hand. And this was a major revelation for me. I previously believed that either I remain ambitious and restless, or I settle down and be content. But now I realize it's not an either-or situation. You don't have to be restless if you aim high. You can be grounded and driven simultaneously. You can drive growth and still feel at peace. You can experience ambition and contentment side by side.

That's what I want to leave here. Vision is not a static image; it's a seed that you cultivate. Growth is not about moving up; it's about moving deep and broad. And achievement is not about results, it's about impact and significance. Along the way, keep learning, keep believing, keep flowing. Your path will be revealed, and when you look back, you'll notice how each little step was part of the bigger narrative.

The perception that ambition and satisfaction are possible simultaneously has been one of the most freeing epiphanies of my existence. I used to believe for years that I was forced to pick between satisfaction and drive. I pictured that to be ambitious was to always be restless, always racing, and that to be satisfied was to settle, to slow, almost to abandon the pursuit. But I know better now. I can be restless and content. I can be ambitious to live even as I live peacefully. The distinction lies in how truthful I am to myself.

When I turn inside out, I know that simplicity comes not from being aware of everything but from having the courage to acknowledge what I really desire and what I really care about. Such inner truthfulness is like a compass. It does not necessarily tell me all the roads in front of me, but it tells me the way I need to go. And when I'm in alignment with myself, even uncertainty isn't so scary.

What I have also realized over time is that asking the correct questions prior to making important decisions is what keeps me balanced. Life always presents us with crossroads, decisions about our careers, relationships, financial gambles, and decisions for personal growth. Those are times of high emotion, times when logic falters and pressure from elsewhere becomes crushing. Those are the times when I depend on the seven questions I have constructed for myself. They are not merely intellectual exercises. They are sifters, beacons that keep me coming back to who I am at my most basic level.

The first question I always pose is: Is this choice consistent with my core values? If a decision appears lucrative, prestigious, or thrilling but at the cost of compromising on honesty, respect, or genuineness, it is not for me.

On paper, it may appear like a golden chance, but if I need to lie, cheat someone, or act against my conscience, then the price is too heavy to pay. I have not learned this from reading books but from experience. Early on in my career, I had been offered something that would give me rapid growth, but it required practices that didn't sit right with me.

I was tempted, of course, who isn't tempted by quick promotions? but something deep within me hesitated. I rejected it, and although I questioned myself for a bit, today I know I made the right decision. Opportunities will always appear and disappear, but allowing your values to be compromised once creates a bad precedent. Values, to me, are the roots of a tree. If the roots are damaged or weak, regardless of how tall the tree reaches, it is always at risk of falling over.

The second question is: am I selecting from purpose or from pressure? I never asked myself that for so long. I would make decisions out on what people told me, out of my ego, or out of fear of missing out. But coaching helped me understand the difference. A purpose-driven decision is one that feels like it comes from the inside.

It thrills me even though it frightens me. A pressure-driven decision is one that feels like it comes from the outside, what others might think, what society demands, what my fear whispers. When I quit my secure corporate career to start coaching, it was not pressure; it was sheer purpose. There was no outside nudge, no fear, no ego. It was a gentle inner tug that instructed, "This is your way now." That is why, in spite of the risks involved, I was able to take that leap.

Contrarily, I have seen instances where individuals, including myself, took actions solely to show something to others. Those choices nearly always result in regret. Purpose gets you through challenging times, but pressure weighs too much and falls.

The third question I ask is: Will this be important five years from now? This is one of the strongest questions because it allows me to step out of the current noise. Life has the tendency to get us caught up in fleeting emotions, excitement, anger, fear, or even fleeting comfort. So many times, we make choices to please the "now," not thinking about the future. But when I sit down and think about how this will be in five years, things shift.

A small discomfort now can mean enormous long-term expansion. A small indulgence now can be long-term regret. For instance, as a parent, I sometimes find myself wondering: Should I lecture my child for something minor? If it is merely playful naughtiness, then no. Five years down the line, no one will care.

But if it is dishonesty or disrespect, then yes, I need to correct it firmly.

Because five years down the line, such habits would define their character. Likewise, at work, agreeing to a project that stretches me might hurt today, but five years down the line, the learning and credibility will count.

The fourth question is: What am I scared of? And is my fear real or imagined? Fear is devious. It lurks in the shadows, dictating our decisions without us even knowing it. Sometimes we shun an experience not because it's incorrect, but because we are scared of failing.

Sometimes we remain in a situation not because it's correct, but because we are scared of change. Fear is most powerful when it is unseen. That is the reason that stating it diminishes its grip. I question myself: what am I really fearing here? Losing money? Failing publicly? Being judged? When I state it, I look to see if it is an actual danger or just a hypothetical situation my brain is creating. I have witnessed the same with my coaching clients. Usually, as soon as they speak the fear aloud, half of its strength is lost. Fear lives in secrecy, but courage in knowledge.

The fifth thing I do is ask: What will it cost me? Every choice has a price tag attached to it, whether you do something or not. Sometimes the act of not choosing is itself a choice, and frequently the most expensive one.

I consider both sides. If I do this, how much will it cost me in time, money, energy, or relationships? If I don't do this, what will that cost me? Often, not doing something costs more.

For instance, when I was thinking about beginning my own practice, it cost me uncertainty and financial risk. But the cost of not acting was remaining trapped in an unfulfilling job where I didn't feel alive. That was a larger cost. This frame of reference serves to make me realize that inaction can at times be more hurtful than risking it.

The sixth question is: what would I tell another person in this same situation? This is a surprisingly good way of detaching from emotion. When I get myself caught up, my feelings obscure my intellect. But if I think of a friend or colleague in the same predicament, what would I say to them? The solution is usually self-evident, down-to-earth, and sage. Then I ask myself: why do I not do the same for myself?

This change of attitude eliminates extraneous emotional static and introduces rational clarity. It reminds me that I already possess the wisdom that I require; I only need to get out of my own feelings in order to access it.

And lastly, the seventh question: can I live with the downside? Every choice has a trade-off. The worst-case scenario is always an option, even if not likely. I prepare myself by asking: if the worst occurs, can I live with it? If the answer is yes, I proceed. If not, I reconsider. For example, when I quit a job, the worst that could have happened was financial hardship for a period of time. Could I have coped with it?

Yes, because I had my savings and loving relatives. That reassured me. But if the negative had outweighed, by example, jeopardizing somebody else's welfare, I would not have done it. Planning for the worst gives me the strength to expect the best.

These seven questions have become my silent mentors. They are not hard and fast rules but guiding stars. They remind me of myself when the noise from outside is deafening. They tell me that clarity is not about being able to prophesise the future but being able to make the right choices today, which are congruent with my true self. The people around me also help to keep me straight, reminding me that it is more than just results but also integrity, purpose, and peace that shape growth and success.

Looking back, I have learned to appreciate the idea that life is more about asking and finding the right questions, more so than having all the right answers. With every question I come to ask myself these seven, I seem to move slowly closer to living a life that is not only successful in the eyes of the world but significant in itself.

Chapter 12: Introspective Prompts to Ignite Your Transformation

When I take a serious look at the legacy, the first thing that comes into my mind does not refer to the offices I have served, the money I have made, or even refer to the change I have caused. Above all of these, I wanted to make people feel good about themselves, about one another, and to have some sort of culture around me.

Individually, I would like to be remembered as a person with a clear sense of purpose, a heart of compassion, and an act of courage. These three words are not a nicely packaged sentence to deliver in a speech; they are the guide I have attempted to hold on to in my own career. Clarity, because during confusion, people seek guidance, and a leader who is unable to communicate the vision has his or her team lost.

Compassion, because results without kindness are nothing. And courage, because every important decision requires the willingness to risk lack of popularity for the sake of doing what is right. If my professional legacy amounts to anything, I hope it is grounded in these three characteristics.

Legacy, though, isn't just about large, obvious accomplishments. It's also about the unseen daily decisions that make us who we are to others. I don't wish to be remembered only as a builder of products, scaler of businesses, and driver of results, although all of those are significant. Winning changes is what I most want to be remembered for having done so in any workplace. To me, transformation has never been just restructuring an organization or adopting a new technology. It has translated into altered perceptions of individuals, an altered attitude to challenges, and a belief in their ability to grow up. That is what I mean by that kind of value that is beyond quarterly toplines and annual objectives.

I will always consider the way I handled the people around me; other workers, people under me, and even those who may have had an issue with me one way or another. I made sure that I accorded people respect. That is not to say I was always soft and gentle. To value someone is also to challenge them. To say, "You can do better than this, and I have enough faith in you to move you into difficult places."

And as much as I criticized someone, it was not to demean him or her but to challenge him or her to view that potential that was in a person but was not in him or her. The same case applied when I gave a team member hard tasks; it was not to torture them but to provide an opportunity to develop. People should have learned they were not fillers in an organizational scheme- they mattered, they were noticed, they were trusted, and they could do much more than they imagined.

A secure environment was the basis for all of this. To me, safety never equated to protecting individuals from punishment, but from judgment and ridicule. When an individual erred, my immediate reaction was never to punish, but to question: why did it occur, and how can we help you so that it doesn't happen again? And that is what psychological safety essentially is- not a negative state of not being held accountable, but a positive state of trust.

I have wanted my teams to feel they were able to take a step, miss, and even fail dramatically without fear of being put to shame. Simply because the fact remains, innovation is never created in fear, but it is achieved in courage, and courage was only established when one had the knowledge that they could not and would not be brought down because they had tried. Should I leave a place in memory, I hope that it would be remembered as a leader who created spaces where people felt cared about, challenged, and free to flourish.

Yet another legacy of mine that I am very, very fond of is leading with principle, not with politics. Politics has never been a language for me. I have never known how to navigate through deception or play games for gain. People will sometimes laugh when I tell them that I do not know how to do politics, but I really mean it. For me, leadership has always been based on fundamental values. Principles, honesty, and fairness have driven my decisions, even when the going was difficult and even when it cost an advantage. Too many times, people have explained to me that politics is inevitable, that survival in big organizations requires a little bit of manipulation. But I never bought into that.

Maybe it made things more difficult for me in some cases, but it also made them cleaner, more true, and more in line with the sort of person I want to be. If I am remembered professionally, I want people to say that I held onto my principles, even when it was uncomfortable, even when it meant less progress. Because integrity might not always get you the short-term win, but it means you never lose the long-term narrative of your life.

Principle-driven leadership also influenced how I made decisions. Decision-making is not often straightforward, particularly when we are in a crisis situation where all solutions seem risky. But during those instances, I relied on my core values as my guiding light. I asked myself questions:

Does this decision uphold the dignity of individuals?

Does it support the long-term well-being, even if the short-term is messy?

Does it contain integrity, or does it call for the compromise of truth?

These questions assisted me in opting for principle rather than convenience, principle rather than expediency. And if there is a lesson that I hope other people take away from my career, it is that the price of principle will feel heavy in the moment, but the dividend of knowing you have not betrayed your values is incalculable.

Leadership and technology have been key themes in my life as well, but I've never viewed them as mechanisms only for efficiency. Efficiency is vital, indeed, but efficiency without purpose is hollow.

My legacy, I hope, will show that I employed technology and leadership not merely to save money or accelerate processes but to have a purposeful effect. Technology is a force multiplier; it will do whatever intent you put into it. If the intent is to make maximum profit, then that's what it will do. But if the intent is to change lives, to open up possibilities, to empower people, then it's something much more significant. I would like to be known as one who wedded technology with leadership to create meaningful impact, someone who employed innovation not for figures but for people.

In retrospect, I see that each milestone, each project, and each leadership position was a chance to create this legacy. In my work with groups, I attempted to convey not only tasks but vision, for clarity inspires people to take action. When I spoke with colleagues in tough talks, I attempted to balance honesty with empathy, for truth unaccompanied by kindness amounts to cruelty.

When I made decisions that pushed my courage, I took a moment to remember that a leader who does not take risks out of fear of condemnation is no leader. These small decisions made each day were really the foundation stones of the legacy I wish to leave behind.

I often consider what others will be saying about me if I am no longer in the room, or years after we last worked together. Will they recall the presentations that I delivered, the goals that I hit, the frameworks that I implemented?

Possibly, but barely. What I want them to remember more strongly is how I made them feel.

Did I make them feel valued?

Did I challenge them in ways that enabled them to expand their potential?

Did they feel secure enough to take risks without fear?

If the answer is yes, then that is the genuine professional legacy I will have left behind.

Of course, legacy cannot be scripted to perfection. It's not all within our power. Human beings are going to see what we do and draw conclusions based on their own path. But what is within our power is the intention we bring to every day, the coherence with which we live out our values, and the integrity with which we appear. And so I strive to live and lead with integrity so that the legacy I want to leave will be one worth leaving.

Whether we like it or not, every interaction is a seed that we are planting in someone else's memory. Years from now, those seeds will germinate into the stories people tell about us. My prayer is that the tales told about me are those of a leader who was direct, kind, and brave; who loved people thoroughly, pushed them to develop, and provided security for them to spread wings; who selected ideals over politics, even when it was difficult; and who employed technology and leadership not for shallow efficiency but for substantial effect.

That is the professional legacy I intend to leave. Not titles, not trophies, not momentary applause, but a lasting memory of values, courage, and purposeful change.

What is efficiency? That was a question that has walked with me through so many phases of my life. For many years, efficiency was being measured in terms of speed, in terms of deadlines achieved, and in terms of output produced. But now that I look back, I see efficiency is not about getting things done fast at all; it is about getting the right things done effectively.

Efficiency to me was never solely about speed; it was about intent. It was about having the ability to harness technology, creativity, and systems to liberate human energy for what really counts: thinking, connecting, dreaming, and creating. If my legacy was that I left behind a platform, or even simply an environment, where meaningful impact was created, then I know I lived with purpose. That, above all else, is how I want to be remembered.

Because if you take a step back from all the noise of accomplishments and awards, the fact is this: people will not often recall how hard or how fast you worked or how many meetings you went to, but they will always recall how you treated them, how you caused them to dream, how you stood with them when they were afraid.

I want to be remembered as that individual, someone that others could go to not only for technical knowledge or direction, but for counsel, for insight, for candid feedback, even when that candor wasn't comfortable. I want to be remembered as the individual who not only produced projects, but also believed. Someone who not only constructs systems but also enables individuals to believe in themselves and what they might create. That type of remembrance, I think, endures much longer than any resume listing or honor.

Legacies are, of course, not constructed exclusively in conference rooms or on project schedules. Personally, as well, there are infinite vectors: family, parents, children, wife, sisters. Each relationship is a universe unto itself, each memory a strand that interweaves into the greater tapestry of who I am. If I had to summarize it, I would want to be remembered as living with heart. That phrase may seem cliché, but it means everything. Living with heart is not just existing, but showing up.

It's not just talking, but listening. It's not just taking, but giving more than you get. And in an age where the world is always urging us to compare ourselves to money, status, or material things, living from the heart is a courageous act. I wish people would be able to say, "He was there. He held true to his principles. He gave more than he got." If I can leave that legacy, then I have lived.

I hope my children, my family, and those closest to me remember me as a person of integrity and empathy. Integrity, because without it, every achievement is hollow. Empathy, because without it, every relationship is shallow. And the truth is, I didn't always get it right. Just like all the rest of us, I've had moments when I didn't listen, when I was absorbed in my own concerns, when I wasn't as fully present as I could have been. But if the totality of my life, the general drift of my steps, pointed towards honesty and kindness, then that's sufficient. That's more than sufficient for many of us.

I would also like to be remembered as having had the courage to reinvent oneself, even if it was to begin again. Reinvention is difficult. It forces you to relinquish identities you've had for years, to confess that the you who worked before no longer works. It means standing on the threshold of not knowing and saying, "I'll keep walking anyway." Few people do that, because it's daunting. It threatens security. But I know now that reinvention is where growth lies in wait. Reinvention is where fear is challenged. If people would remember me as a person who had the courage to shed worn-out skins and step into new forms of himself, I would count that as the greatest compliment.

And in this transformation, I don't merely wish to be remembered as a professional who got things done. I want to be remembered by my kids as a father who loved with all his heart, who was imperfect but genuine, who attempted to lead them not through sermonizing but by example through his own behavior. I want my wife to recall me as a man who held her ground, who was her partner in joy and adversity.

I want my sisters to recall me as a brother who cared, who watched over them, whose triumphs were theirs as well. I want my closest friends to recall me as a man who gave them straight talk when they needed it, and silent support when words could not suffice. In brief, I would like to be remembered as more than a title or a position, but rather as a human being who loved and lived sincerely.

If I had to summarize it in a sentence, I want people close to me to be able to say, "He walked his way with courage, and in doing so, he helped others walk theirs too." That to me is legacy. Not the buildings, not the bank account, not the claps. Legacy is the ripple of fearlessness you leave in others. Legacy is when they decide to move one step ahead because they once saw you move one. Legacy is when they take strength from remembering your tale.

And if readers, or anyone who ever encountered my experience, were to recall one thing from all of it, what is it? The one thing that I would leave them with is this: you don't have to have it all together. Nobody does. Life isn't about knowing, it is about wondering. It isn't about perfection; it is about trying. Stay honest. Stay curious. Keep coming with heart, even when the outcomes are uncertain, even when the path is longer than you imagined. Because the truth is, the journey itself forms you, astounds you, and expands you beyond your wildest dreams.

There will be times when you are adrift. There will be times when the world compares you to unattainable expectations. There will be days when you glance around and question whether you are doing enough. But in those times, return to your values. Return to ownership. Return to serving others along the way. Because when you do, you build a life that is not only successful on the outside, but rich with meaning on the inside. That is impact. That is legacy.

And legacy isn't a stirring speech at your departure or your name etched in marble. Legacy is in the small things that people continue to bring you into their lives. It's in your kid mimicking something that you always said. It's in your co-worker recalling that one bit of wisdom you shared with them years before. It's in your family, remembering how you persevered when it was difficult. Legacy exists in memory, in repeat, in the subtle ways your impact lasts long after you're dead.

I think real efficiency, real effectiveness, is when the structures you put in place last beyond you, but also when the love and bravery you provided ring on beyond your time. That's what I want to be remembered by. Not for the emails fired off, but for the hearts you've touched. Not for the tempo, but for the reason. Not for the noise, but for the substance. That is the narrative I hope my life shares, and that is the narrative I leave with you.

The Journey Never Ends: And The Learning Continues...

To the final thoughts that I wish to share with you. If you have stuck with me through these reflection stories and lessons, thank you. I recognize that attention is the most precious currency of today's world, and the fact that you chose to follow me through these words, I do not take lightly. What I would like to leave with you is this: your path is yours alone.

It will not resemble anyone else's, and it shouldn't. There will be times when it will appear that everyone else is moving ahead while you're standing still, and there will be times when you will think you've sprouted ahead only to fall a little afterward. They're all rhythms of life.

There will be highs that convince you the whole universe is urging you on, lows that challenge all of the strength you possess, about-turns that require you to unlearn and begin anew, and moments of stillness when nothing appears to be happening yet everything within you is reshaping itself. My request to you is to accept them all, even the messy, painful, inconvenient moments, for it is in those very moments that the seeds of the growth you will eventually need are planted.

If there is one thing I have learned over time, and I have learned it deeply, it is that showing up with honesty is greater than showing up with perfection. Curiosity trumps certainty. Kindness trumps cleverness. Values are longer-lasting than tactics. Assisting others to rise will always lead you farther than attempting to ascend on your own. And learning, persistent learning, will be your biggest strength, whatever your discipline, whatever you have already done.

Life has a tendency to remove illusions and remind you that the world continues to turn and that the only way to best keep up is to continue to learn. A specific life lesson that I would like to mention at the end is to continue learning and growing, because **Seekhna Band toh Jeetna Band**. This basic yet powerful idea, if you stop learning, you stop winning, has been the foundation of my life.

I have witnessed this fact repeating itself again and again. Regardless of how experienced you get, regardless of how good you become at what you do, regardless of how sure you feel of yourself and your abilities, life will make you humble. It will place you in a setting where, suddenly, you are the least knowledgeable of all. It will deliver into your hands a problem you can't fix with your old solutions.

It will expose you to individuals who will challenge your perspective and tell you that knowledge is endless. And every time, you are being asked to begin again, to resume the thread of wonder and proceed ahead with it. It is not punishment; it is a blessing. It tells you that life still has enough faith in you to grow.

This philosophy has kept me humble in times of success for me. It has taught me that the claps are momentary, but the wisdom is permanent. In times of failure, it has given meaning, since failure does not hurt so much once you start viewing it as uncut precious stones for insight. In times of doubt, when I could not discern the way ahead, it has reminded me that growth is always within reach if I will remain inquiring. And in the long periods of tedium where nothing dramatic was happening, it has been the quiet discipline that honed me gradually, almost imperceptibly.

I have had many different hats on my career path: technologist, leader, advisor, and coach. Each was associated with its own set of responsibilities, its own obstacles, its own persona. None of those labels has propelled me forward. Labels are fleeting. Roles change. Praise wears off. What has propelled me ahead is not a title or a job but the learner's mentality.

The mindset that each adversity is a classroom, each error is a message, and each individual you meet is a teacher. I can not stress it enough: never underappreciate what a person can teach you.

At other times, the lesson will be from a mentor who has preceded you, at other times from a fellow traveler who is experiencing the same struggle, and at other times from a stranger whose narrative intersects with yours for a brief moment. Listen well, and you will always discover something you can learn.

As I look back, I see that every crossroads in my life arrived because I was open to learning. When chances came, learning empowered me to say yes even though I was not ready. When failures happened, learning provided me with resilience to say this is not the end, but only the start of something new. When fears crept in, learning provided me with clarity to go ahead despite the fear. And when happiness came, learning provided me with the gratitude to notice it.

So bear in mind, as you read these pages, this much, which is, never cease to learn. Read extensively, listen attentively, be not afraid to ask questions, and be surprised. Be curious about things outside your discipline, outside your comfort zone, outside that which is practical. Since you never know what morsel of knowledge, what insight, what story, will be the spark to set off your next chapter.

And with learning, don't forget kindness. There is a lot of noise in the world about ambition and competition, but kindness gives meaning to your passage through it. Lift up those who need lifting whenever you can, because success grows when you share it. Be true to yourself, because your values will survive every fad.

Be authentic, not flawless, because people are sustained by honesty more than they are dazzled by perfection. And most importantly, grow with intention. Growth for growth's sake can leave one empty, but purposeful growth makes every step worthwhile.

And as I draw this to a close, I do do more than I wish to leave to you: I hope, I hope, that you will at the same time think of what I wish. I wish you the courage to face the unknown, the humility to keep learning, the power to rise again after failures, and the prudence to see even simple things as beautiful.

I wish you, be strong enough to make your own history and not to be like other people. I hope for you moments of great connection, where you are seen and where you see people. And I pray for you the grace to leave behind something greater than what was left for you.

Because in the end, that's all that will matter. Not the titles, not the things, not the temporary adoration. What will matter is who you have become, how you have treated other people, what you have learned, and what you have given back. Perfection was never the aim. Authentic, actual, receptive to being, this is what is to be done.

So keep moving, with wonder in your back pocket and compassion in your heart. Keep climbing, not because of yourself but because of people who pass at your side. Keep growing, since the time you stop is the time you stop benefiting.

And most importantly, never stop believing that your story, with all its twists and turns, is exactly the story that the world is expecting. That is what I keep with me, and what I would like to impart.

Verses Kindler Publication

Reach us through our website -

https://www.verseskindlerpublication.com/

For more information visit our Instagram or Facebook page.

www.ingramcontent.com/pod-product-compliance
Lightning Source LLC
Chambersburg PA
CBHW061344230926
51848CB00004B/526
* 9 7 8 9 3 4 9 5 3 2 7 5 5 *